INSIDE

LANGUAGE · LITERACY · CONTENT

Acknowledgments

Grateful acknowledgment is given to the authors, artists, photographers, museums, publishers, and agents for permission to reprint copyrighted material. Every effort has been made to secure the appropriate permission. If any omissions have been made or if corrections are required, please contact the Publisher.

Photographic Credits

Cover (front): Royal Bengal Tiger, Ranthambore National Park, Rajasthan, India, Danita Delimont. Photograph © Danita Delimont/Gallo Images/Getty Images.

Acknowledgments continue on page 199.

For product information and technology asistance, contact us at **Cengage Learning Customer & Sales Support, 1-800-354-9706**

For permission to use material from this text or product, submit all requests online at **www.cengage.com/permissions** Further permissions questions can be emailed to **permissionrequest@cengage.com**

National Geographic Learning | Cengage Learning
1 Lower Ragsdale Drive
Building 1, Suite 200
Monterey, CA 93940

Cengage Learning is a leading provider of customized learning solutions with office locations around the globe, including Singapore, the United Kingdom, Australia, Mexico, Brazil, and Japan. Locate your local office at **www.cengage.com/global**.

Visit National Geographic Learning online at **ngl.cengage.com**
Visit our corporate website at **www.cengage.com**

ISBN: 978-12857-34682 (Practice Book)
ISBN: 978-12857-34590 (Practice Book Teacher's Annotated Edition)

ISBN: 978-12857-67987 (Practice Masters)
Teachers are authorized to reproduce the practice masters in this book in limited quantity and solely for use in their own classrooms.

Printed in the United States of America
Print Number: 15   Print Year: 2024

INSIDE

LANGUAGE · LITERACY · CONTENT

NATIONAL GEOGRAPHIC LEARNING | CENGAGE Learning

Contents

Unit 4

Unit 5

Unit 6

Contents, continued

Unit 1 Launch

Name _____

Mind Map

Use the Mind Map to show how people in the community rely on one another.
As you read the selections in this unit, add new ideas you learn about working
as a team.

I Could Help

▶ **Language: Tell What May Happen**

▶ **Grammar: Verbs:** *May, Might, Could*

Complete each sentence. Tell about the job Jim could have.
Use words from the box.

may meet	might be	could take
could go	might carry	could fight
might save	may drive	may rescue

1. I ____might save____ lives.

2. I _____ the ambulance.

3. I _____ people to the hospital.

4. I _____ boxes.

5. I _____ to different places.

6. I _____ nice people.

7. I _____ a firefighter.

8. I _____ fires.

9. I _____ people.

What Time Is It?

▶ **Vocabulary: Time**

▶ **Language: Tell What May Happen**

A. Look at each clock. Write the time. Use words from the box.

| ten to five | nine o'clock | eleven fifteen | noon | two thirty | quarter after six |

1.

It's ___nine o'clock___ .

2.

It's _____ .

3.

It's _____ .

4.

It's _____ .

5.

It's _____ .

6.

It's _____ .

B. Look at each picture above. Tell what may happen at that time.

7. Mrs. Patch ___may teach children about other birds_____ .

8. The mail carrier _____ .

9. The firefighters _____ .

10. The crossing guard _____ .

11. The delivery man _____ .

12. The doctors _____ .

We Have to Help!

▶ Grammar: Phrases with *Have to* and *Need to*

Use a verb to complete a phrase with *have to* or *need to*.

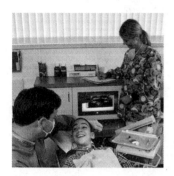

have to	+	verb

They **have to work** together.
She **has to help** the dentist.

Use *has* with *he, she,* or *it*.

need to	+	verb

They **need to wear** masks.
He **needs to use** tools.

Use *needs* with *he, she,* or *it*.

Complete each sentence. Circle the correct form of *have to* or *need to*.

1. They (**need to**) / **needs to** ___ fix the road.

2. They ___ **need to / needs to** ___ help each other.

3. They ___ **has to / have to** ___ wear hard hats.

4. She ___ **need to / needs to** ___ stop traffic.

5. He ___ **has to / have to** ___ deliver the mail.

6. He ___ **need to / needs to** ___ check the address.

7. It ___ **has to / have to** ___ show the person's name.

8. He ___ **need to / needs to** ___ take the letter to the right place.

Name _____

What Is Your Job?

▶ Grammar: Possessive Adjectives

Possessive adjectives tell who or what owns something.

Adjective	Example
my	I help **my** patients.
your	**Your** friend Ben is one of my patients.
his	**His** sister visited him yesterday.
her	She talked to **her** brother.
its	This bed moves. It rolls on **its** wheels.
our	We will take Ben to **our** operating room.
your	Will you visit **your** friend later?
their	His parents are here to see **their** son.

Read each sentence. Add the missing adjective.

1. We have many patients in _____our_____ hospital.

2. I am a nurse. I enjoy helping _____ patients.

3. An ambulance is coming. I hear _____ siren.

4. This young man fell off _____ bike and hurt his leg.

5. "Does _____ leg feel better now, Jim?"

6. "Yes, _____ leg feels fine," he says.

7. His parents are here. They want to
   see _____ son.

8. Jim's mom is glad. _____ son
   will be all right.

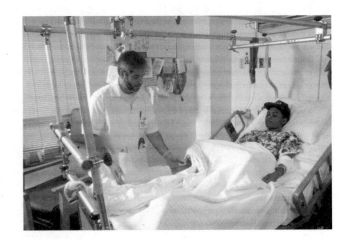

Language Development

Identify Cause and Effect

▶ Sum It Up

Read the paragraph. Look for the main cause and its effects. Complete the cause-and-effect chart.

> **Stormy Night**
>
> There was a huge storm that night. Rain poured down and the wind roared. In the valley, trees fell to the ground. In the mountains, the storm caused mud to slide down a hill. In town, the power went out. Everywhere, there were floods.

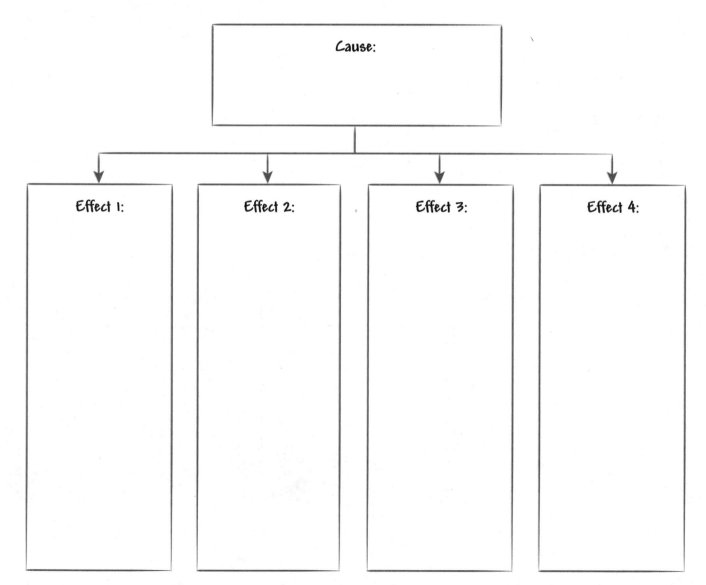

Cause:

Effect 1:

Effect 2:

Effect 3:

Effect 4:

Name _____

High Frequency Words, Part 1

A. Read each word. Then write it.

1. been _____

2. four _____

3. sound _____

4. caused _____

5. between _____

B. Read each sentence. Find the new words in the box. Write the words on the lines.

6. My little brother is _____four_____ years old.

7. He has always _____ fast.

8. One time, he walked away without making a _____ .

9. Kento _____ Mom a lot of worry.

10. Now he stays _____ Mom and me!

High Frequency Words, Part 2

A. Read each word. Then write it.

1. could	_____
2. almost	_____
3. life	_____
4. often	_____
5. never	_____

B. Read each sentence. Find the new words in the box. Write the words on the lines.

6. Kento ____almost____ always holds Mom's hand.

7. One day Mom said he _____ walk without her.

8. Kento has been lost only once in his _____ .

9. He _____ gets lost anymore.

10. He _____ tries to stay near Mom.

Name _____

Words with Long *i*

A. Name each picture. Write the name.

1.

   pie
   _____

2.

   _____

3.

   _____

4.

   _____

5.

   _____

B. Now read the story. Circle the words with long *i*. Write them in the chart. Write each word one time.

(Pie) for Tonight

Li helps out in the kitchen. Today Mom is making a pie. Li washes and dries his hands. Then he rolls out Mom's dough. He puts the dough into a bright red pan. He makes it lie flat. Next Mom cuts up apples. Li mixes them with just the right amount of sugar. Mom finishes up. Then they put the pie in the oven.

The finished pie is a beautiful sight! The crust is light and flaky. The family will eat the pie tonight.

6. _____pie_____	9. _____
7. _____	10. _____
8. _____	11. _____
	12. _____
	13. _____

Name _____

Words with Long *i* or Long *u*

A. Name each picture. Write the name.

1.

____pie____

2.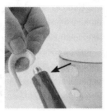

_____

3.

_____

4.

_____

5.

_____

6.

_____

B. Now read the story. Circle the words with long *i* or long *u*. Write them in the chart. Write each word one time.

The (Right) Thing

Nam often helps at the senior center. He

thinks it's the right thing to do. He helps in

many ways. He serves pie. He brings in books

and takes back the books that are (due.) In art

class, Nam helps people cut and glue things.

He gets the paints—bright red, yellow, blue.

Four nights a year, the center has a big show.

Nam wears a suit and tie. The shows are

always great!

7. ____right____	12. ____due____
8. _____	13. _____
9. _____	14. _____
10. _____	15. _____
11. _____	

Name _____

Build Reading Fluency

► Expression

A. When you read, use good expression. Watch for commas, question marks, and other punctuation to help you.

> "I have never seen flames so high and so bright!" Yamada said. "It's true! I almost lost my life!"

B. Listen to the story. When the reader shows excitement, circle the exclamation mark. When the reader pauses, circle the comma. When you hear the reader's voice go down, circle the period.

Example: He called the fire station. Soon, he heard the sound of fire trucks.

Hot Crumbs Cause Fire

A fire woke Kenji Yamada at 4 a.m. He called the fire station. Soon, he heard the sound of fire trucks.

"I have never seen flames so high and so bright!" Yamada said. "It's true! I almost lost my life!" When he tried to throw water on the fire, he burned four fingers. Paramedics treated him.

Firefighters asked what caused the fire. At first, Yamada didn't have a clue. He went to bed between 10 p.m. and 11 p.m. Then, he smelled smoke. It came from his kitchen. "I think it was something in my trash," he sighed.

C. Now read the story to a partner. Use the marks you made to read with good expression.

Learn Key Vocabulary

Name _____

Dog Detectives: Key Vocabulary

A. Study each word. Circle a number to rate how well you know it. Then complete the chart.

Rating Scale	**1** I have never seen this word before.	**2** I am not sure of the word's meaning.	**3** I know this word and can teach the word's meaning to someone else.

▲ Dogs help **police officers rescue** people.

Key Words	Check Understanding	Deepen Understanding
❶ **earthquake** (**urth**-kwāk) *noun* Rating: 1 2 3	Wind and rain can cause an **earthquake**. Yes No	What happens during an earthquake? _____ _____ _____
❷ **emergency** (ē-**mur**-jen-sē) *noun* Rating: 1 2 3	A large forest fire is an **emergency**. Yes No	Tell about an emergency that you have had or that you know about. _____ _____ _____ _____
❸ **life** (līf) *noun* Rating: 1 2 3	You will grow and change during your **life**. Yes No	What would you like to accomplish in your life? _____ _____ _____

Name _____

Some dogs are trained to help **rescue** people in a water **emergency**.

Key Words	Check Understanding	Deepen Understanding
❹ rescue (**res**-kyū) *verb* **Rating:** 1 2 3	A lifeguard might **rescue** a drowning person. **Yes** **No**	When might a firefighter rescue someone? _____ _____ _____
❺ police officer (pō-**lēs o**-fi-sur) *noun* **Rating:** 1 2 3	A **police officer** helps sick pets get well. **Yes** **No**	Name some jobs that a police officer does. _____ _____ _____ _____

B. Use at least two of the Key Vocabulary words. Tell why you think some
dogs like to help people.

_____

_____

_____

Name _____

Plan a Friendly Letter

Fill in the FATP chart.

PREWRITE

1. **Collect Ideas** Fill in this chart with writing ideas.

FATP Chart

Form: _____

Audience: _____

Topic: _____

Purpose: _____

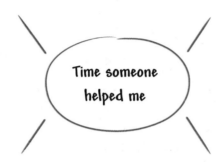

Time someone helped me

2. **Choose a Topic** Now circle the best idea. That will be your topic. Add the topic to your FATP chart.

3. **Organize Ideas** Write what you did. Write details that tell what happened.

Detail Chart

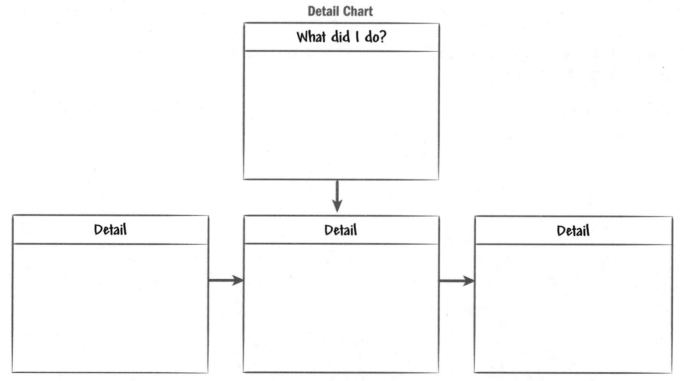

What did I do?

| Detail | Detail | Detail |

Draft a Friendly Letter

Write a letter about how someone helped you. Use your detail chart.

1. Write the **date** in your heading. The heading goes in the top right-hand corner.

2. Write the **greeting**. Write *Dear* followed by the person's name.

3. Write the **body** of your letter. Include a **topic sentence** and **detail sentences** to tell who helped you and what happened.

4. Write a **closing** for your letter. Sign your name.

Revise a Friendly Letter

PRACTICE REVISING

Read the friendly letter. Make sure there are details that tell what happened.
Mark the changes. To add text, use this mark: ∧.

April 18, 2008

Dear Suki,

I learned how to play some computer games, but it wasn't easy. At first, I tried to read a

book and play on my own. It didn't work! I didn't know what I was doing wrong. So I asked Mrs.

Green. She helped me. She showed me how to play them.

Your friend,

Mari

REVISE YOUR DRAFT

Read your paper aloud to a partner. Mark your changes on p. 15.

Edit and Proofread a Friendly Letter

CHECK FOR CAPITAL LETTERS

Proofread the sentences. Correct errors in capitalization.
Mark your changes.

1. My best friend is anna griffin.

2. every Saturday, anna and I go to our garden.

3. Our garden is on park street.

4. It is a neighborhood garden started by mr. posada.

5. Mr. Posada came each saturday to show us how to tend the garden.

6. he can make anything grow!

PRACTICE EDITING AND PROOFREADING

Edit and proofread this friendly letter. Mark your changes.

> may 26, 2008
>
> dear Grandma
>
>   I have been busy with my project. I went to the parker Animal
> Shelter with my friend. miss lopez told us the shelter needs
> help with invitations to the fund-raiser. I am helping Miss Lopez
> and their friends make invitations. Mine job is to find all the
> dog owners. Then I put the rite names on the list and gloo the
> address labels on the envelopes. It is fun! I can't wait to help at the
> fund-raiser!
>
>   Love
>
>   Matt

Editing and Proofreading Marks	
∧	Add.
ℐ	Take out.
⋏	Replace with this.
⬭	Check the spelling.
≡	Capitalize.
/	Make lowercase.
¶	Make a new paragraph.

Checklist
- ❑ Commas
- ❑ Spelling
- ❑ Capitalization

EDIT AND PROOFREAD YOUR FRIENDLY LETTER

Now edit and proofread your friendly letter on p. 15.

Unit 2 Launch

Mind Map

Use the Mind Map to show how you can make a difference. As you read the selections in this unit, add new ideas you learn about how to make the world a better place.

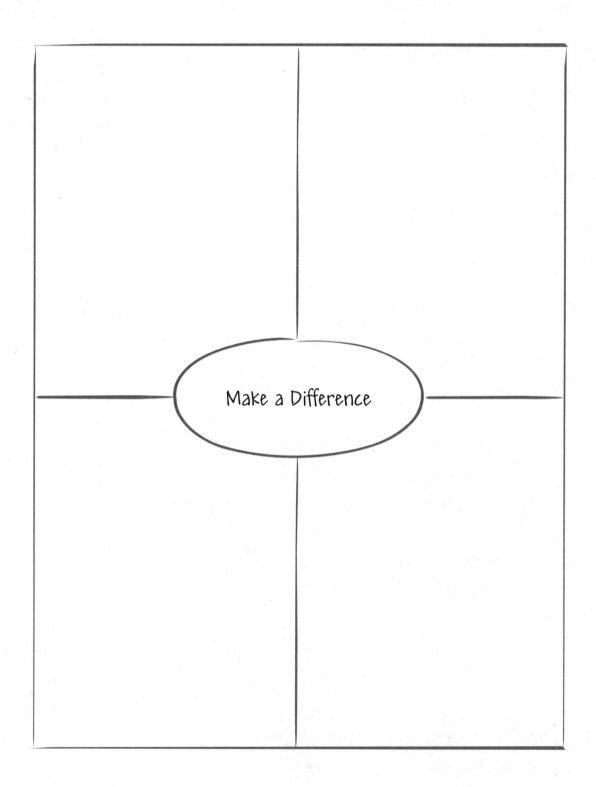

Tell Me About It

▶ **Language: Give Information**

▶ **Grammar: Irregular Past Tense Verbs**

Read each sentence. Change the verb in dark print to the past tense. Write the sentence.

1. I **am** lost and alone.

   I was lost and alone. _____

2. I **feel** confused and worried.

   _____

3. A girl **speaks** to me.

   _____

4. She **comes** with me to the bus.

   _____

5. I **meet** her after school.

   _____

6. We **make** plans for the next day.

   _____

7. I **am** not lonely any more.

   _____

8. We **are** best friends!

   _____

Language Development

We Help at the Playground

▶ **Vocabulary: Direction Words**

▶ **Language: Give Directions**

A. Study the picture. Complete each sentence. Use a direction word from the box.

up	around	down	across	into

1. Janis walks ___around___ the sandbox.

2. Bill steps _____ the sandbox.

3. Kira goes _____ the slide.

4. Rico and Brad walk _____ the bridge.

5. May helps Jess go _____ the ladder.

B. Read each sentence. Find the places in the picture above. Write the directions.

6. Tell how to get from the ground to the top of the slide.

   Stand at the bottom of the ladder. Go up the steps. _____

7. Tell how to get from the sandbox to the swings.

   _____

8. Tell the people on the bridge how to get to the slide.

   _____

Language Development

Name _____

Make a Change

▶ **Vocabulary: Civil Rights**

▶ **Language: Express Wants and Feelings**

A. These people want to save an old house. What can they do? Complete the sentences. Use words from the box.

banner	protest	ballot	print	letters	sign	vote	Internet

1. The people can ___protest___ .

2. They can use a _____ or a _____ .

3. Adults can _____ .

4. They can use a _____ in an election.

5. People can write _____ .

6. They can _____ their ideas in a newspaper.

7. They can publish ideas over the _____ , too.

B. Answer each question. Write a complete sentence.

8. How do the people feel about the house?

_____

9. What do the protesters want others to do?

_____

Language Development

They Gave People Hope

► Grammar: Irregular Past Tense Verbs

These verbs have special forms to tell about the past.

Frederick Douglass

Present	Past	Example
think	thought	Frederick Douglass **thought** slaves should be free.
lead	led	He **led** the movement to end slavery.
go	went	He **went** across America.
give	gave	He **gave** strong speeches.
speak	spoke	He **spoke** about equal rights.
see	saw	Many people **saw** him and agreed with him. In 1865, Congress passed a law to end slavery.

Complete each sentence. Use the past tense of the verb in dark print.

1. Eleanor Roosevelt ____thought____ all people should have
   (think)
   the same rights.

2. She _____ a movement to get fair treatment for
   (lead)
   people everywhere.

3. Eleanor _____ around the world.
   (go)

4. She _____ with the leaders of many countries.
   (speak)

5. She _____ important speeches.
   (give)

6. People _____ her and agreed with her ideas.
   (see)

Eleanor Roosevelt

Comprehension

▶ Identify Sequence

Read about important events in civil rights. Then put the events in order.
Use them to make a time line of civil rights.

Time Line of Civil Rights

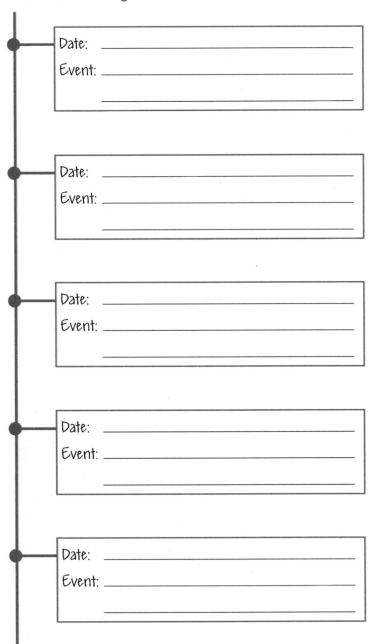

Date: _____

Event: _____

_____

Date: _____

Event: _____

_____

Date: _____

Event: _____

_____

Date: _____

Event: _____

_____

Date: _____

Event: _____

_____

Events in Civil Rights

• In 1965, César Chávez helped farmworkers.

• Martin Luther King, Jr., gave a famous speech in 1963.

• In 1920, women got the right to vote.

• A law ended slavery in 1865.

• In 1964, a new law gave all Americans equal rights.

Name _____

High Frequency Words, Part 1

A. Read each word. Then write it.

1. country	_____
2. called	_____
3. lived	_____
4. house	_____
5. now	_____

B. Read each sentence. Find the new words in the box. Write the words on the lines.

6. This word means almost the same as **home**.

_____ house _____

7. This word rhymes with **cow**.

_____

8. These words are past tense verbs.

_____   _____

9. This word has two syllables.

_____

10. This word is the opposite of **later**.

_____

High Frequency Words, Part 2

A. Read each word. Then write it.

1. American _____

2. would _____

3. know _____

4. should _____

5. also _____

B. Read each sentence. Find the new words in the box. Write the words on the lines.

6. These two words rhyme.

____would____   ____should____

7. This word has four syllables.

_____

8. This word has **so** in it.

_____

9. This word always begins with a capital letter.

_____

10. This word rhymes with **show**.

_____

Language and Literacy

Words with *R*-controlled Vowels

A. Name each picture. Write the name.

1.

   barn

2.

   _____

3.

   _____

4.

   _____

5.

   _____

6.

   _____

7.

   _____

8.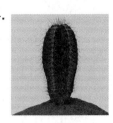

   _____

B. Now read the story. Circle the words that go in the chart.
Write them in the chart. Write each word one time.

(Storm) Watch

Carrie always enjoys watching a good storm.

She lives on a farm with a red barn and fields

of corn. When the storm blows, the rain whips

across the fields and lightning fills the sky.

Sometimes, part of the corn is torn straight

from the stalks by the wind. During one storm,

hail fell on the car and it set off the car alarm

horn.

Carrie likes a good storm far better than fair

weather. But she prefers to watch it from inside

the house!

9. ___ storm ___	13. _____
10. _____	14. _____
11. _____	15. _____
12. _____	16. _____
	17. _____

Name _____

Words with *R*-controlled Vowels

A. Name each picture. Write the name.

1.

    _____car_____

2.

    _____

3.

    _____

4.

    _____

5.

    _____

6.

    _____

7.

    _____

8.

    _____

B. Now read the story. Circle the words that go in the chart. Write them in the chart. Write each word one time.

(Part) of a Team

Melvin is part of a rescue team. When sea birds are hurt after a storm or an oil spill, his team takes them to a yard. First they clean off the oil and dirt. Melvin holds the birds and turns them as he washes off the oil. He stays at the yard from morning until night. It is a hard job, but it is important. When the birds chirp in a happy way, Melvin is also happy. He knows that the birds may survive.

⭐	🧑
9. ____part____	16. _____
10. _____	17. _____
11. _____	18. _____
	19. _____
🎺	👧
12. _____	20. _____
13. _____	21. _____
14. _____	22. _____
15. _____	

Language and Literacy

Words with *R*-controlled Vowels

A. Name each picture. Write the name.

1.

_____pair_____

2.

_____

3.

_____

4.

_____

5.

_____

6.

_____

7.
_____

8.

_____

B. Now read the story. Circle the words that go in the chart. Write them in the chart. Write each word one time.

The Race

Jill put her (hair) back in a band. She was ready to start the race. She had worked hard. Last time, she had come in third. This time, she hoped to come in first.

Jill came out of the first turn in third place. The air cooled her face. Her shirt flapped in the wind. She felt the burn in her muscles.

She passed the last pair of runners. Jill crossed the finish line. She was a star!

9. ___hair___	15. _____
10. _____	16. _____
11. _____	17. _____
12. _____	18. _____
13. _____	19. _____
14. _____	

Words with *R*-controlled Vowels

A. Name each picture. Write the name.

1.

steer

2.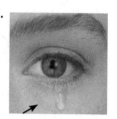

_____

3.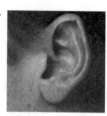

_____

4.

_____

5.

_____

6.

_____

7.

_____

8.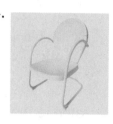

_____

B. Now read the story. Circle the words that go in the chart.
Write them in the chart. Write each word one time.

A Great Guy

Lee always ⟨cheers⟩ people up. One year,

when I was sick, he gave me a toy deer. It was

so funny. It had a wig with long hair and a pair

of sunglasses. Last year, Lee planted tomatoes

near his house. He gave my mom a bag of big,

bright tomatoes. Lee also helps a family in

another country. He sends them socks to wear.

He brings stuffed bears to kids in Children's

Hospital.

9. ___cheers___	13. _____
10. _____	14. _____
11. _____	15. _____
12. _____	16. _____

Build Reading Fluency

▶ Phrasing

A. When you read, pause between groups of words that go together.

> When Nadja was a girl, / ethnic groups in Bosnia / started a war. // Nadja was not safe, / even in her house. //

B. Listen to the story. When you hear a short pause, write a / . When you hear a long pause, write // .

Example: She also published / two books. //

> **Kids Are Helping Kids**
>
> Nadja helped kids in Bosnia. When Nadja was a girl, ethnic groups in Bosnia started a war. Nadja was not safe, even in her house. Kids lived in fear. A lot of them were hurt. Naja started a radio show. She sang on the air to give children courage. She also published two books. They tell how hard it is to live through a war. She hopes her books will help end fighting in the world.

C. Now read the story to a partner. Use the marks you made to read groups of words together.

Learn Key Vocabulary

Striving for Change: Key Vocabulary

A. Study each word. Circle a number to rate how well you know it. Then complete the chart.

▲ Martin Luther King, Jr., gave speeches about giving people **rights**.

Rating Scale	**1** I have never seen this word before.	**2** I am not sure of the word's meaning.	**3** I know this word and can teach the word's meaning to someone else.

Key Words	Check Understanding	Deepen Understanding
❶ protest (**prō**-test) *verb* **Rating:** 1 2 3	People **protest** against things they like. Yes No	What is something you might protest against? _____ _____ _____ _____
❷ right (rīt) *noun* **Rating:** 1 2 3	American adults have the **right** to vote. Yes No	What rights should all people have? _____ _____ _____ _____
❸ sign (sīn) *noun* **Rating:** 1 2 3	A **sign** has information you can read. Yes No	Name some places you can find signs. _____ _____ _____ _____

Name _____

At one time, **women**, like the ones shown here, did not have the **right** to **vote**. ▶

Key Words	Check Understanding	Deepen Understanding
❹ **vote** (vōt) *verb* **Rating:** 1 2 3	No one can **vote** in an election. **Yes** **No**	Why is it important to vote? _____ _____ _____ _____
❺ **women** (wi-mun) *noun* **Rating:** 1 2 3	Mothers, aunts, and sisters are **women**. **Yes** **No**	Describe two women you admire. _____ _____ _____ _____

B. Use at least two of the Key Vocabulary words. Tell about a right that you would fight for if it were taken away from you.

_____

_____

_____

Plan a Personal Narrative

Fill out the FATP chart.

FATP Chart

Form: _____

Audience: _____

Topic: _____

Purpose: _____

PREWRITE

1. **Collect Ideas** Record your writing ideas in this chart.

What I Saw	What I Did and How I Felt

2. **Choose a Topic** Now circle the best idea. It will be your topic. Add the topic to your FATP chart.

3. **Organize Ideas** List the events in order. Then write the events in the chart below.

Story Plan

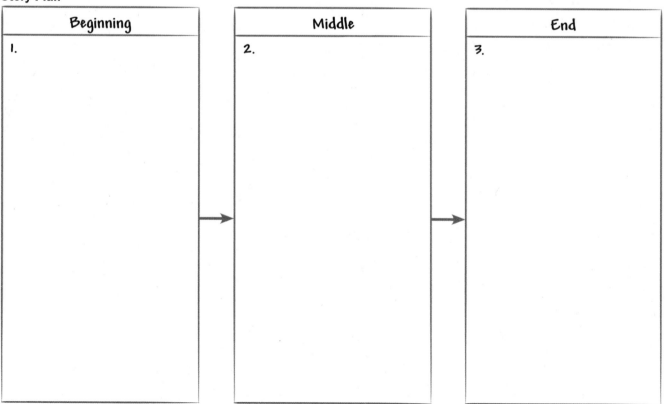

Beginning	Middle	End
1.	2.	3.

Name _____

Draft a Personal Narrative

Tell a story about how you made a difference. Use your organizer.

1. Write the **beginning**. The beginning is what happened **first**.

2. Write the **middle**. Tell what you did and how you felt.

3. Write the **end**. The end is what happened **last**. Tell how you felt.

Revise a Personal Narrative

PRACTICE REVISING

Read this personal narrative. Make a list of the order of events. Then mark
your changes. To move words, use this mark: ⤴⃝.

Order Of Events

1. _____

2. _____

3. _____

4. _____

5. _____

> I helped my little sister many times.
>
> Last year, I helped her with math homework.
>
> When she was a little baby, I helped feed her.
>
> When she first came to school, I showed her where things were.
>
> Now I am helping my little sister learn how to help others.
>
> Last month, my baby brother was born.

6. What is unclear? _____

REVISE YOUR DRAFT

Read your paper aloud to a partner. List any changes that you need to make.
Then, mark your changes.

_____

_____

Name _____

Edit and Proofread a Personal Narrative

CHECK FOR CAPITAL LETTERS

Proofread the sentences. Correct errors in capitalization.
Mark your changes.

1. My name is maria hayes.

2. I make a difference by volunteering at the senior center
   on saturdays.

3. My sister, anne, volunteers with me.

4. anne also volunteers after school on wednesdays.

5. mom says that next year I can go on wednesdays, too.

6. anne and I love to help at the senior center.

7. I think that saturdays are the best day of the week!

Editing and Proofreading Marks	
∧	Add.
℘	Take out.
⌐	Replace with this.
◯	Check the spelling.
≡	Capitalize.
/	Make lowercase.
¶	Make a new paragraph.

PRACTICE EDITING AND PROOFREADING

Edit and proofread this personal narrative. Mark your changes.

Checklist
- ❏ Past tense verbs
- ❏ Spelling
- ❏ Capitalization

> Last saturday, I go to the supermarket with mom. I see mr.
> jaresh. He helped me with my math homework last thursday. mr.
> jaresh slipped and falled. He was hut. I got help for Mr. jaresh.
> On sunday, Mom and I goed to mr. jaresh's house. Mr. Jaresh
> was fine. He had crutches! I got a cad in the mailbox on tuesday.
> It was a thank-you cad from mr. jaresh. I send a card back and
> said thank you for your help with math. I helped someone who
> helped me.

EDIT AND PROOFREAD YOUR PERSONAL NARRATIVE

Now edit and proofread your personal narrative on p. 34.

Name _____

Mind Map

Use the Mind Map to show how to help animals. As you read the selections in this unit, add new ideas you learn about what animals need and how they can be helped.

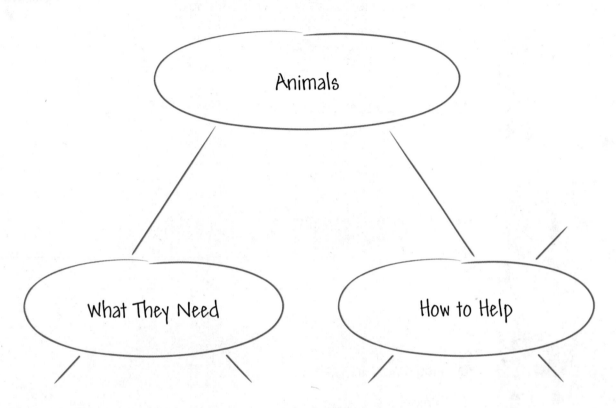

What Is Your Opinion?

▶ **Language: Give Your Opinion**

▶ **Vocabulary: Opinion Words**

Read the opinion. Then write your own opinion. Use words from the box.

1.

Everyone should care for Earth.

My Opinion: _I believe that everyone should care for Earth._ _____

_____

2.

We must clean up our water.

My Opinion: _____

_____

3.

You should pick up trash.

My Opinion: _____

_____

4.

We should stop air pollution.

My Opinion: _____

_____

5.

We must protect the forest.

My Opinion: _____

_____

Language Development

What Lives Around the Water?

▶ **Vocabulary: Animals and Habitats**

▶ **Language: Describe Places**

A. Name what you can see in each place. Use the chart.

Seashore			Pond		
salt water	jellyfish	seal	frog	fish	turtle
starfish	seagull	crab	fresh water	duck	beaver

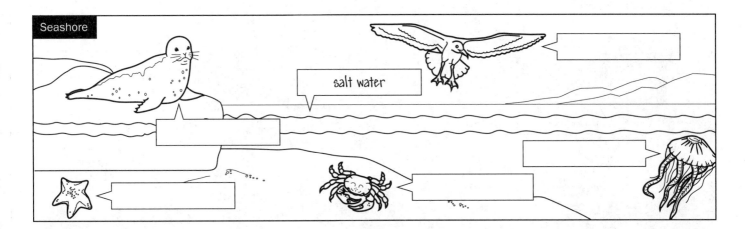

B. Complete each sentence. Describe the plants and animals above. Add an adjective from the box.

1. I see a ___big seal___ at the seashore.

   There is a _____ in the water.

2. I see a _____ in the pond.

   There is a _____ in the water.

Adjectives
little
big
small
large

Language Development

Name _____

Life in the Forest

▶ **Vocabulary: Plants and Habitats**

▶ **Language: Make a Suggestion**

A. Name the things in the pictures. Use words from the box.

branch	flower	tree	trunk
petal	soil	stem	undergrowth

Forest

tree

B. What can you and your friends do in the forest? Make some suggestions.

1. Let's ___take pictures with our cameras___ .

2. Would you like to go _____ ?

3. We could look _____ .

4. Why don't we _____ ?

Name _____

Describe the Earth

▶ Grammar: Sensory Adjectives

Adjectives can tell what something is like.

An adjective can tell how something looks.

The Joshua tree is **tall**.

An adjective can tell how something sounds.

A **loud** coyote is near the tree.

An adjective can tell how something feels.

The desert is **hot**.

Complete each sentence. Add an adjective from the box. Tell how each thing looks, sounds, or feels.

Looks		Sounds		Feels	
tall	small	quiet	noisy	hard	hot

1. The ___*hot*___ sun shines on the desert.

2. A _____ cactus grows there.

3. The rocks feel hot and _____ .

4. A _____ snake slides through the sand.

5. A _____ bird chirps at the snake.

6. A _____ rabbit stops to rest.

Identify Details

▶ **Sum It Up**

Read about Sam's day at the seashore. Then complete the data chart below.

Sam's Day at the Seashore

Sam went to the seashore to study plants and animals. First, he walked
on the white sand. There he saw a large, red crab. Then he walked to the
water. He saw green seaweed. He saw two large fish. Next, Sam looked up in
the sky. He saw a seagull. Sam wrote about all these things in his notebook.
It was a good day.

Data Chart

Order	Place	Animals
1	sand	

Name _____

High Frequency Words, Part 1

A. Read each word. Then write it.

1. mountains _____

2. oil _____

3. found _____

4. because _____

5. few _____

B. Answer the question.

6. Which words begin with the letter **f**?

_____ found _____   _____

C. Work with a partner. Follow the steps.

• Read aloud each new word in the box.

• Your partner writes the words.

• Have your partner read the words to you.

• Now you write the words on the lines below.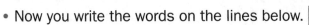

• Read the words to your partner.

7. _____

8. _____

9. _____

10. _____

11. _____

High Frequency Words, Part 2

A. Read each word. Then write it.

1. try   _____

2. over   _____

3. away   _____

4. why   _____

5. story   _____

B. Answer the question.

6. Which words rhyme with **by**?

_____try_____   _____

C. Work with a partner. Follow the steps.

- Read aloud each new word in the box.

- Your partner writes the words.

- Have your partner read the words to you.

- Now you write the words on the lines below.

- Read the words to your partner.

7. _____

8. _____

9. _____

10. _____

11. _____

Name _____

Types of Syllables

A. Name each picture. Read the two words. Circle the word that names the picture.

1.

marker / (market)

2.

letter / winter

3.

perfume / person

4.

under / ladder

5.

garden / garter

6.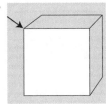

timber / corner

7.

hammer / summer

8.

butter / pepper

B. Now read the story. Then read each word in the chart. Write the syllables in the word.

My Sister Meg

My sister Meg should live on a farm and drive a tractor. She loves to grow things! She gets perfect seeds at the market and plants them in our garden. She plants peppers for Dad and turnips for Mom. Gram asks for butter beans. Meg plants a few things for herself: plums and peas. We all help harvest what she grows. Then we cook supper. Food from the garden always tastes better!

Words	Syllables	
9. sister	sis	ter
10. perfect	____	____
11. garden	____	____
12. peppers	____	____
13. turnips	____	____
14. butter	____	____
15. harvest	____	____
16. supper	____	____

Language and Literacy

Build Reading Fluency

▶ Phrasing

A. When you read, pause between groups of words that go together.

> That is why it is so hard / to see a white-tailed deer. // Many people try.//

B. Listen to the story. When you hear a short pause, write a / . When you hear a long pause, write // .

Example: In the winter,/ when there is snow,/ it has gray-white fur.//

> **Animals in the Wild**
>
> You might have heard a story about a white-tailed deer. It is an animal that lives in the forest and has a short tail. It has brown fur in the summer. In the winter, when there is snow, it has gray-white fur. That is why it is so hard to see a white-tailed deer. Many people try.
>
> The male deer has antlers that drop off in the winter and grow again when winter is over. These new antlers soon grow hard and sharp.

C. Now read the passage to a partner. Use the marks you made to read groups of words together.

Learn Key Vocabulary

Animal Ecosystems: Key Vocabulary

A. Study each word. Circle a number to rate how well you know it. Then complete the chart.

Rating Scale	**1** I have never seen this word before.	**2** I am not sure of the word's meaning.	**3** I know this word and can teach the word's meaning to someone else.

▲ Raccoons need to live in a **forest ecosystem** to **survive**.

Key Words	Check Understanding	Deepen Understanding
❶ **ecosystem** (ēk-ōh-sis-tum) *noun* **Rating:** 1 2 3	Plants and animals in a park are in the same **ecosystem**. Yes　　　No	Describe parts of the ecosystem you live in. _____ _____ _____ _____
❷ **forest** (for-est) *noun* **Rating:** 1 2 3	You will not see plants and animals in a **forest**. Yes　　　No	Name some animals and plants that live in a forest. _____ _____ _____ _____
❸ **pond** (pond) *noun* **Rating:** 1 2 3	You can find sharks in a **pond**. Yes　　　No	What might you do at a pond? _____ _____ _____ _____

Name _____

Plants like the corn plants here need **soil** to survive.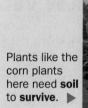

Key Words	Check Understanding	Deepen Understanding
❹ **soil** (soil) *noun* Rating: 1 2 3	Plants need **soil** to grow. Yes No	What do you do to soil when you plant something? _____ _____ _____ _____
❺ **survive** (sur-**vīv**) *verb* Rating: 1 2 3	People can **survive** for months without water. Yes No	Name at least two things people need to survive. _____ _____ _____ _____

B. Use at least two of the Key Vocabulary words. Tell about the living and nonliving things in your ecosystem.

_____

_____

_____

Name _____

Plan a Fact-and-Opinion Article

Fill out the FATP chart.

Form: _____

Audience: _____

Topic: _____

Purpose: _____

PREWRITE

1. **Choose an Animal** List animals that you want to write about. Choose an animal. Circle your choice.

Animals

2. **Gather Facts** Use books and the Internet to find facts about your animal. Write facts in the first column of the chart.

Facts	Opinions

3. **Write Your Opinions** In the second column of the chart, write what you think or believe about the animal.

Name _____

Draft a Fact-and-Opinion Article

Tell facts and opinions about the animal. Use ideas from your chart.

1. Name the animal. Write the name on the title line.

2. Write a **sentence** identifying the animal that you researched.

3. Write about your animal.
   - Write **facts**. Use your research. Include **adjectives**.
   - Write **opinions**. Use opinion words, like *think* or *should*.

Revise a Fact-and-Opinion Article

PRACTICE REVISING

Read this fact-and-opinion article.

The Giant Panda

The giant panda lives in China. The panda is unique. It is the most beautiful animal in China. It has a white head. It has patches around its eyes and on its ears and shoulders. Giant pandas eat only plants. They can chew on bamboo shoots and roots for twelve hours a day. Pandas are becoming rare. Hunters kill them. Bamboo forests are disappearing. What will happen to the pandas? It is time to save the pandas!

How can the writer make it better? Revise the paper. Mark your changes. _____

_____

_____

REVISE YOUR DRAFT

Read your paper aloud to a partner. Mark your changes on p. 50. To add a word or phrase, use this mark: ∧.

Edit and Proofread a Fact-and-Opinion Article

	Editing and Proofreading Marks
∧	Add.
℘	Take out.
⋏	Replace with this.
◯	Check the spelling.
≡	Capitalize.
/	Make lowercase.
¶	Make a new paragraph.

CHECK FOR COMMAS

Proofread the sentences. Check for commas in a series.
Mark your changes.

1. Coral reefs are found in many places. Australia Florida, and
   Southeast Asia are famous for their coral reefs.

2. Coral reefs are home to more species than forests lakes or mountains.

3. Fish, mollusks and urchins live in coral reefs.

4. Coral reefs are shaped like cabbages, tabletops tree trunks, and wrinkled brains.

5. Storms, people and global warming are destroying coral reefs.

6. We should explore study, and protect the coral reefs.

PRACTICE EDITING AND PROOFREADING

Edit and proofread this fact-and-opinion article. Mark your changes.

I think elephants are a lot like people. Earth's largest land
animals live in a family. An elephant family is ruled by an older
female. There are usually six twelve, or twenty membrs in a
family. Older females, younger females and young males are in a
family. As males grow older, they leave the family and join other
males. Elephants have large sensitive, and powerful ears. They
can hear sounds from far off. They use their trunks to sniff at
the wind. Oders help them know what they hear. Elephants are
endangered. Hunters kill them for ivory, their lands are being
developed and farmers kill them if the elephants eat their crops. I
belive it is everyone's job to help save Earth's largest animals.

Checklist

❑ Adjectives
❑ Spelling
❑ Commas

EDIT AND PROOFREAD YOUR FACT-AND-OPINION ARTICLE

Now edit and proofread your fact-and-opinion article on p. 50.

Mind Map

Use the Mind Map to show how to learn about the past. As you read the selections in this unit, add new ideas you learn about how we can study the past.

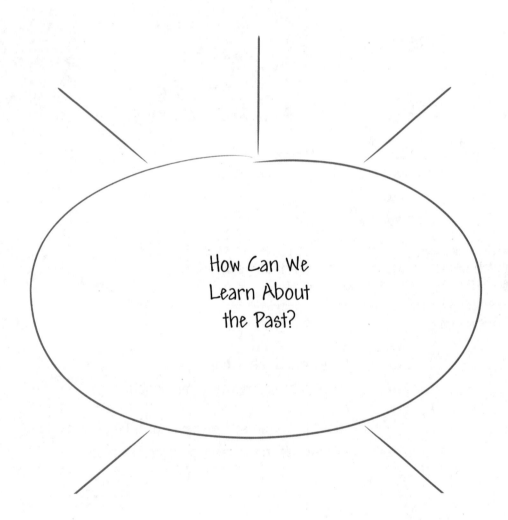

How Can We
Learn About
the Past?

Language Development

How We Learn About the Past

▶ **Vocabulary: Historical Records**

▶ **Language: Make Comparisons**

A. Complete each sentence. Tell about the picture. Use words from the box.

newspaper	historian	diary	history book	photographs

1. In a _____ diary _____ ,
you can read about what a
person's life was like in the
past.

2. A _____
has _____
that make the news come
alive.

3.
A _____
is written by a
_____ .

B. Complete each sentence. Compare the historical records.

4. Both a _____ newspaper _____ and a _____ give
facts about events.

5. A _____ reports events as they happen, but a
_____ reports events after they have happened.

6. A _____ tells about the events in one person's life, but a
_____ tells about events in the lives of many people.

Language Development

Name _____

Person, Place, or Thing?

▶ Grammar: Nouns

A noun names a person, place, or thing.

Rosie the Riveter

Rosie the Riveter stood for all the <u>women</u> who worked in
    person   **people**

<u>factories</u> in <u>America</u> during <u>World War II</u>.
  things   **place**   **thing**

Read each sentence. Tell if the underlined word is a person, place, or thing.

1. During <u>World War II</u>, many American men had to go to war.   _____thing_____

2. They went to <u>Europe</u>, Africa, and Asia.   _____

3. They had to leave their jobs in the <u>factories</u>.   _____

4. Soon <u>women</u> went to work in the factories.   _____

5. They wanted to help <u>America</u> win the war.   _____

6. Some workers helped build <u>airplanes</u>.   _____

7. Other women helped build <u>ships</u>.   _____

8. The American <u>soldiers</u> were thankful for their work.   _____

9. The <u>workers</u> were proud to help their country.   _____

10. They proved that women can do any <u>job</u>.   _____

American women helped build ships and airplanes.

Language Development

Name _____

The 1940s: What We Did

▶ **Grammar: Present and Past Tense Verbs**

A verb changes to show when an action happens.

Use a present tense verb to tell what happens now.

> Today kids **listen** to CDs.

Use a past tense verb to tell what happened in the past. To form the past tense, you usually add **-ed**.

> In the 1940s, kids **listened** to records.

Study the verbs in the box. They have a special form to show the past tense.

Present	Past
leave	left
are	were
say	said

Complete each sentence. Use the correct form of the verb from the box above.

Present

1.

Today families _____*say*_____ ,
"Let's watch TV."

Past

In the 1940s, they often _____ ,
"Let's listen to the radio."

2.

Today a worker _____ milk at the store.

In the 1940s, a worker _____ milk at someone's house.

3.

Now CDs _____ popular.

In the 1940s, records _____ popular.

Language Development

Make Comparisons

► Sum It Up

A. Read about Tanya. Tell how you and Tanya are alike. Tell how you and Tanya are different. Use the chart.

> Tanya lived through a war. She wrote me a letter about it. She said there was no school for a year. Sometimes it was hard to get food. Her dad was in the army. He was gone for months. Her family had no money for clothes or other important things. But the war is over now, and Tanya says life is much better!

Comparison Chart

About Tanya	About You
Tanya lived through a war.	

B. Read each question. Write the answer.

How are you and Tanya the same?

1. We both _____ .

2. We both _____ .

3. We both _____ .

How are you and Tanya different?

4. Tanya _____, but I _____ .

5. Tanya _____, but I _____ .

6. Tanya _____, but I _____ .

Language and Literacy

High Frequency Words, Part 1

A. Read each word. Then write it.

1. news   _____

2. words   _____

3. much   _____

4. along   _____

5. question   _____

B. Read the clue. Write the word in the chart. Then write the word again in the sentence.

What to Look For	Word	Sentence
6. has **ew**	n e w s	I send my friend Ted my ___news___ .
7. begins with **w**	__ __ __ __ __	I write lots of _____ .
8. means "a lot"	__ __ __ __	I like him so _____ .
9. ends with **ng**	__ __ __ __ __	I went _____ to say goodbye.
10. ends with **tion**	__ __ __ __ __ __ __ __	I ask him one _____ .

Language and Literacy

High Frequency Words, Part 2

A. Read each word. Then write it.

1. before   _____

2. miss   _____

3. example   _____

4. ever   _____

5. back   _____

B. Read the clue. Write the word in the chart. Then write the word again in the sentence.

What to Look For	Word	Sentence
6. has an **x**	e x a m p l e	Ted is an ___example___ of a true friend.
7. tells when	__ __ __ __ __ __	He left _____ summer.
8. ends with **ss**	__ __ __ __	I _____ my friend.
9. has a **v**	__ __ __ __	He's the best friend I _____ had.
10. ends with **ck**	__ __ __ __	When will you come _____ ?

Language and Literacy

Words with *y*

A. Read each word. Tell if the letter *y* is a vowel or a consonant.

1.
yard
consonant

2.
twenty
_____

3.
sky
_____

4.
happy
_____

5.
year
_____

6.
yarn
_____

B. Read the story. Circle the words with *y*. Write the words in the chart. Write each word one time.

(Why) I Admire Raoul Wallenburg

My class read about World War II. In one story, a man risked his life to save others. He could not be happy while other people suffered so much. He gave a lot of lucky people passports so that they could escape. He helped other people find places to hide. By the end of the war, he had helped 100,000 people.

7. ___why___   10. ___story___

8. _____   11. _____

9. _____   12. _____

Language and Literacy

Plurals: *y* + *s*, *y* to *i* + *es*

A. Read each sentence. Change the word in dark type to name more than one.

1. I have many _____ hobbies _____ .
   (hobby)

2. On some _____ , I make model planes from World War II.
   (day)

3. My _____ like to help me.
   (buddy)

4. We eat lunch on _____ as we work.
   (tray)

5. We tell each other _____ about the planes.
   (story)

6. We pretend the planes are still up in the _____ .
   (sky)

B. Now read the story. Circle the plurals that end in *-ys* and *-ies*. Write each word in the chart. Then write the root word.

Dad's Favorite Hobby

My dad has many (hobbies.) The hobby he likes best is history. He likes to read about England and other countries in World War II. Sometimes he tells me stories about those days. Dad has other ways to learn about history. For example, he collects old things, like newspapers, stamps, and coins from the forties.

Word that Ends in *-ys* or *-ies*	Root Word
7. _____ hobbies _____	hobby
8. _____	_____
9. _____	_____
10. _____	_____
11. _____	_____
12. _____	_____

Language and Literacy

Build Reading Fluency

▶ Expression

A. Some sentences tell something. Other sentences show strong feeling.

> This sentence tells something. It ends with a period.
>
>   We explain news stories in easy words.
>
> This sentence shows strong feeling. It ends with an exclamation mark.
>
>   I say YES!

B. Listen to the different kinds of sentences.

> **Can Kids Make History?**
>
> Misako says:
>
> Good question! I say YES! More than ever before, kids are making history. In my school, we have a radio show just for kids. We explain news stories in easy words. We help kids understand the news. That way, young people will not miss what's happening in the world.
>
> Mary says:
>
> Hello, Misako. A kid's radio show is a great example of how to make history! I have my own Web site. It tells people where to send food for needy children. My Web site makes me happy. I know I'm helping babies get a good start in life.

C. Now read the sentences to a partner. See how your reading improves!

Learn Key Vocabulary

Name _____

Our Government: Key Vocabulary

A. Study each word. Circle a number to rate how well you know it. Then complete the chart.

Rating Scale	**1** I have never seen this word before.	**2** I am not sure of the word's meaning.	**3** I know this word and can teach the word's meaning to someone else.

▲ People created buildings like the Washington Monument to celebrate the **freedom** of having their own **government**.

Key Words	Check Understanding	Deepen Understanding
❶ **declared** (dē-**klaird**) *verb* **Rating:** 1 2 3	Americans **declared** they had a new nation in 1776. Yes No	Name something a president might have declared. _____ _____ _____ _____
❷ **freedom** (**frē**-dum) *noun* **Rating:** 1 2 3	Abraham Lincoln helped African Americans gain **freedom**. Yes No	Name one specific kind of freedom that Americans have. _____ _____ _____ _____
❸ **government** (**guv**-urn-ment) *noun* **Rating:** 1 2 3	The United States **government** is made up of elected officials. Yes No	Name two ways the government helps you. _____ _____ _____ _____

Key Vocabulary, continued

These people protest to **declare** what they want the **government** to do. ▶

Key Words	Check Understanding	Deepen Understanding
❹ laws (laws) *noun* **Rating:** 1 2 3	When people break **laws**, they always go to jail. **Yes** **No**	Why are laws important? _____ _____ _____ _____
❺ power (pow-ur) *noun* **Rating:** 1 2 3	Americans have the **power** to vote for a president. **Yes** **No**	Name a power that voters have. _____ _____ _____ _____

B. Use at least two of the Key Vocabulary words. Tell about a law that you would make and why it would be important for people to follow.

_____

_____

_____

Writing Project

Plan a Comparison Paragraph

Fill out the Form, Audience, and Purpose in your FATP chart.

FATP Chart

Form: _____

Audience: _____

Topic: _____

Purpose: _____

1. **Collect Ideas** Circle the decade that you will learn about:

   1890s   1900s   1910s   1920s   1930s

   1940s   1950s   1960s   1970s

   Write the decade as the topic in your FATP chart.

2. **Collect Facts** Collect facts and pictures (or add drawings) about the decade that you chose. Fill in the decade and facts below.

Facts	Pictures

3. **Make a Plan** Copy the facts from above into column 1 below. In column 2, write how life today compares with the fact about the past.

Comparison Chart

Decade: _____	Today

Name _____

Draft a Comparison Paragraph

Write a paragraph comparing life in the past with life today. Use the facts in your chart.

1. Find or draw pictures of the decade you will write about and pictures of life today.

Decade: _____

Today

2. Write a title and **topic sentence** telling which decade you will compare to today.

3. Write sentences to explain how life is the same or different. Tell about what people did and how they do it today.

   · Use present and past tense verbs.

   · Use the correct pronouns.

   · Use words that compare.

Name _____

Revise a Comparison Paragraph

PRACTICE REVISING

Read and revise this comparison paragraph. Make a list of what is being compared. Then mark your changes. To move text, use this mark: ⟲.

1. _____

   and _____

2. _____

   and _____

3. _____

   and _____

In some ways, life in the 1950s and life today are the same.

In the 1950s, families spent a lot of time doing activities together.

In other ways, life is different. Watching television in the 1950s is

like today in one way. Today, family members spend more time using

personal computers and music players on their own. In the 1950s, people

spent almost as much time watching television as people do today.

4. What is unclear? _____

5. Mark your changes. To move words, use this mark: ⟲.

REVISE YOUR DRAFT

Read your paper aloud to a partner. Mark your changes on p. 66.

Edit and Proofread a Comparison Paragraph

Editing and Proofreading Marks	
∧	Add.
℘	Take out.
⁀	Replace with this.
⬭	Check the spelling.
≡	Capitalize.
╱	Make lowercase.
¶	Make a new paragraph.

CHECK FOR COMMAS

Proofread the sentences. Correct errors in using commas.
Mark your changes.

1. In the 1940s, many people rode trains walked, or rode airplanes.

2. Today, even more people ride trains drive or ride airplanes.

3. Lots of people in the 1940s rode trains to visit different people, places or events.

4. Today many cities have modern trains or subway systems that people ride to go to work go to school or visit friends.

5. Cars in the 1940s were slow. Today, cars are faster safer, and last longer.

6. Transportation today is easier faster and safer than it was in the 1940s.

PRACTICE EDITING AND PROOFREADING

Edit and proofread this comparison paragraph. Mark your changes.

Checklist

❏ Past tense verbs
❏ Spelling
❏ Commas

> Toys were different in the 1930s than they are today. In the 1930s, toies were made of china wood metal, tin, and lead. Toys were meant to last for a long time. Today most toys are made of plastic. Meny of the toys in the 1930s were homemade. When these toys broke they could be fixed easily. When today's toys break they are often thrown away. People just buy new toys. In the past, children played with things they found such as ropes boxes and sticks. Today children buy most of their toys in stores. However, children today are just like children in the 1930s. They also use toys to have fun play and use their imaginations. Toyz may change, but the way children enjoy them will not.

EDIT AND PROOFREAD YOUR COMPARISON PARAGRAPH

Now edit and proofread your comparison paragraph on p. 66.

Mind Map

Use the Mind Map to show where to find stories and what the different parts of stories are. As you read the selections in this unit, add new ideas you learn about stories.

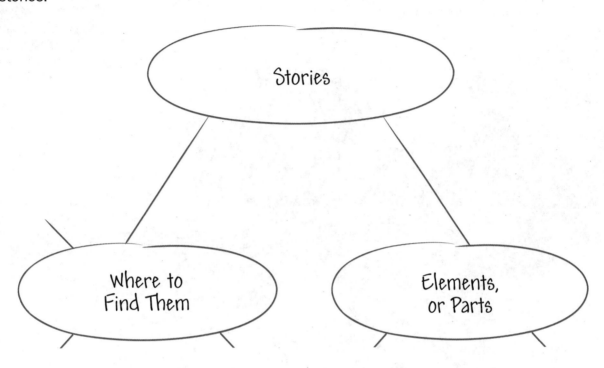

Language Development

What Should the Characters Do?

▶ **Language: Ask for and Give Advice**

▶ **Vocabulary: Story Elements**

A. Study the picture. Complete the chart.

> ### What's in a Story?
>
> A **character** is a person or an animal in a story.
>
> The **setting** is the time and place that the story happens.
>
> The **plot** is what happens in the story from the **beginning** to the **middle** to the **end**.

Story Elements

Characters		
superhero	the ocean	A man swims in the ocean.
shark	early in the morning	A monster chases him.
monster		A shark comes.
swimmer		A superhero saves the man.

B. Write about the story. What should the characters do?
Give them advice. Use the chart.

1. Superhero: _____

2. Shark: _____

3. Swimmer: _____

Language Development

Two Sides of the Story

▶ **Vocabulary: Opposites**

▶ **Language: Ask for and Accept a Favor**

A. Name each character. Use words from the box.

| tall giant | brave girl | good fairy | short elf | old woman | strong bear |

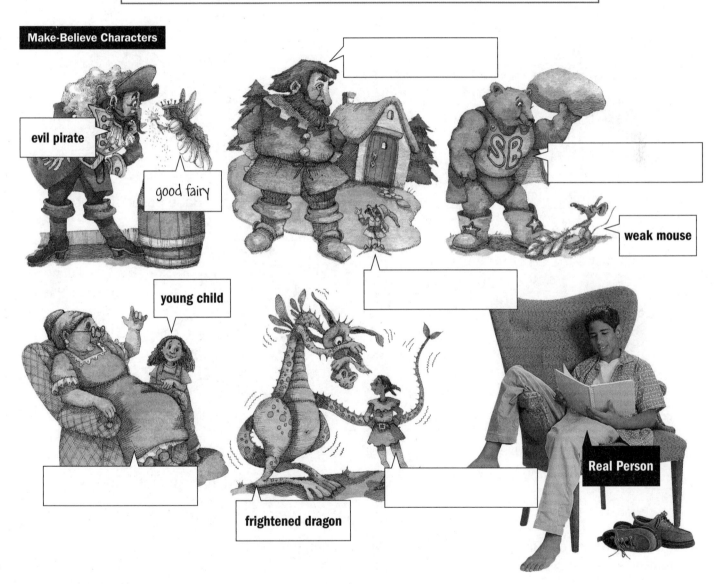

Make-Believe Characters

evil pirate

good fairy

weak mouse

young child

frightened dragon

Real Person

B. The young child asks the old woman for a favor. Complete their sentences.

1. **Young Child:** Can you _____ ?

   Old Woman: Yes, I _____ .

2. **Old Woman:** I will _____ .

   Young Child: _____ ! You are very nice!

A Time and a Place for Everything

▶ **Vocabulary: Phrases for Times and Places**

▶ **Language: Describe Actions**

A. Complete each sentence. Use words from the box.

From 6:00 to 7:00 a.m.   At night   up the mountain   across the river

1.

__From 6:00 to 7:00 a.m._____ ,

Babe ate grass in the valley.

2.

At 10:00 a.m., Babe pulled a wagon

_____ .

3.

After lunch, Babe took boxes

_____ .

4.

_____ ,

Babe rested in the forest.

B. When and where did Babe go? Make up a setting to complete each sentence.

5. ___At 8:00 a.m._____ , Babe went ___around the lake_____ .

6. _____ , Babe went _____ .

7. _____ , Babe went _____ .

8. _____ , Babe went _____ .

Name _____

A Genie at His Command

▶ Grammar: Commands

A command tells someone to do something.

A command can end with a period or an exclamation mark.

> Listen to my command.
>
> Go outside.
>
> Put the trash away!

Jeff wants to give the genie some commands. Choose the correct word to complete each command. Add a period or an exclamation mark at the end.

1. _____Get_____ bikes for my friends ___!___
   (Get / Go)

2. _____ me a box of jewels _____
   (Bring / Grow)

3. _____ some music for me _____
   (Play / Paint)

4. _____ new sneakers on my feet _____
   (Sing / Put)

5. _____ a big house for my mother _____
   (Plant / Build)

6. _____ me a story _____
   (Take / Tell)

7. _____ a sandwich for me _____
   (Do / Make)

8. _____ me to the mall _____
   (Put / Take)

Identify Character Traits

▶ **Sum It Up**

Read the story. Then make a character map. List the characters' actions. List what the actions tell about the characters.

> ### The Magic Rice Pot
>
> A long, long time ago, two men lived in India. Navjot was very poor. The goddess Durga felt sorry for him. She gave him a magic rice pot. It was always full of rice. Navjot gave deep thanks to Durga. With this pot, he was content.
>
> But one day an innkeeper visited. He saw the pot. He tricked Navjot into giving it to him.
>
> The goddess Durga was watching. "I have a better pot for you," she told the innkeeper. The innkeeper took the pot. But when he opened it, evil spirits rose up. They began to beat him.
>
> "We will not leave until you give back the pot!" the spirits cried. What could the man do? He gave the magic pot back to Navjot.

Character Map for "The Magic Rice Pot"

Character	What the Character Does	What the Character is Like
Durga	She gives Navjot a magic rice pot.	kind
Navjot		
Innkeeper		

Language and Literacy

Name _____

High Frequency Words, Part 1

A. Read each word. Then write it.

1. as   _____

2. sentence   _____

3. idea   _____

4. plants   _____

5. into   _____

B. Read each sentence. Find the new words in the box. Write the words on the lines.

6. This word is first in ABC order.

   _____ as _____

7. This word starts with **s**.

   _____

8. This word is something you think of.

   _____

9. This word names things that grow.

   _____

10. This word is the opposite of **out of**.

    _____

High Frequency Words, Part 2

A. Read each word. Then write it.

1. until _____

2. but _____

3. seemed _____

4. each _____

5. made _____

B. Read each sentence. Find the new words in the box. Write the words on the lines.

6. This word is the last in ABC order.

_____ until _____

7. These 2 words have a **u**.

_____ _____

8. This word starts with an **s**.

_____

9. This word has **ea**.

_____

10. This word starts with an **m**.

_____

Words with *oi* and *oy*

A. Name each picture. Write the name.

1.

boy

2.

_____

3.

_____

4.

_____

5.

_____

6.

_____

B. Now read the story. Circle the words with *oi* or *oy*. Write them in the chart. Write each word one time.

One Boy's Story

I know a boy who enjoys stories. One day he wrote his own story. It went like this.

It was a boiling hot day. A little boy went outside to plant some peppers. As he dug, he found an old toy soldier. He set the toy aside. Then he put seeds into the moist soil. When he was done, he set the toy next to the seeds. The soldier would join him in watching the seeds. They would share the joy of growing peppers.

7. _____boy_____	11. ____boiling____
8. _____	12. _____
9. _____	13. _____
10. _____	14. _____

Language and Literacy

Words with *oi*, *oy*, *ou*, and *ow*

A. Read each word. Which picture goes with the word? Write its letter.

1. boil *G*
2. couch ___
3. owl ___
4. crown ___
5. house ___

6. cloud ___
7. boy ___
8. crowd ___
9. coin ___
10. points ___

11. proud ___
12. soil ___
13. mouse ___
14. frown ___
15. toys ___

A.

B.

C.

D.

E.

F.

G.

H.

I.

J.

K.

L.

M.

N.

O.

B. Read each word. Find the word or words above that have the same vowel sound and spelling. Write the words on the lines.

16. join

_____ boil _____

_____

_____

_____

17. joy

_____

_____

18. loud

_____

_____

_____

_____

_____

19. clown

_____

_____

_____

Language and Literacy

Words with *oo* and *ew*

A. Name each picture. Write the name.

1.

___pool___

2.

_____

3.

_____

4.

_____

5.

_____

6.

_____

B. Now read the story. Circle the words with *oo* or *ew*. Write them in the chart. Write each word one time.

A Winter (Stew)

What do you do on cool winter evenings? Do you watch the moon? Do you dream of summer days in the swimming pool? Do you read in your room?

I love to make a good stew. I put in a few vegetables. I add meat and broth. The stew bubbles for a while. Soon it seems ready. I scoop up a little. I taste it. It's done! The taste is always surprising and new.

7. ___cool___	13. ___stew___
8. _____	14. _____
9. _____	15. _____
10. _____	
11. _____	
12. _____	

Name _____

Words with *oo*, *ew*, *au*, *aw*, *al*, and *all*

A. Read each word. Which picture goes with the word? Write its letter.

1. mall   _H_   2. saw   ___   3. broom   ___   4. salt   ___   5. screw   ___

6. hawk   ___   7. author   ___   8. moon   ___   9. stew   ___   10. hall   ___

11. draw   ___   12. boots   ___   13. laundry   ___   14. pool   ___   15. ball   ___

A.    B.    C.    D.    E.

F.    G.    H.    I.    J.

K. 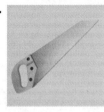   L.    M.    N.    O.

B. Read each word. Find the words above that have the same sound and spelling. Write the words on the lines.

16. cool   _broom_

17. awful   _____

18. small   _____

_____   _____   _____

_____   _____   _____

_____

19. chew   _____

20. haunted   _____

21. also   _____

_____   _____

Language and Literacy

Build Reading Fluency

▶ Expression

A. Some sentences tell something. Other sentences show strong feeling.

> This sentence tells something. It ends with a period.
>
> > He liked the room.
>
> This sentence shows strong feeling. It ends with an exclamation mark.
>
> > "Welcome to your new home, Paul!"

B. Listen to the different kinds of sentences.

> **New Home**
>
> "Welcome to your new home, Paul!" Mr. Brown handed Paul a story on tape and a set of keys to his room.
>
> "Thank you! I love stories on tape!" said Paul. He liked the room. It had many plants. "I have an idea. Please, come in and join me for tea."
>
> "I can't tonight," said Mr. Brown, "but I hope you enjoy the tape. It's a great story."
>
> Paul nodded. He liked the author very much! He had read every sentence in every one of her stories.

C. Now read the sentences to a partner. See how your reading improves!

Learn Key Vocabulary

Stories from Greece: Key Vocabulary

A. Study each word. Circle a number to rate how well you know it.
Then complete the chart.

Rating Scale	**1** I have never seen this word before.	**2** I am not sure of the word's meaning.	**3** I know this word and can teach the word's meaning to someone else.

▲ This **ancient** vase shows Pegasus, a **character** from a Greek myth.

Key Words	Check Understanding	Deepen Understanding
❶ ancient (ān-shunt) *adjective* **Rating:** 1 2 3	**Ancient** houses were made of glass and steel. Yes No	Name an ancient story. _____ _____ _____ _____
❷ characters (kair-ek-turz) *noun* **Rating:** 1 2 3	You will find **characters** in a comic strip. Yes No	Name a movie and one main character. _____ _____ _____ _____
❸ plot (plot) *noun* **Rating:** 1 2 3	The **plot** of a story tells what happens to characters. Yes No	Retell the plot of one of your favorite stories. _____ _____ _____ _____

Key Vocabulary, continued

Name _____

This sculpture shows gods that are **characters** in Greek myths.
▶

Key Words	Check Understanding	Deepen Understanding
❹ content (kun-**tent**) *adjective* **Rating:** 1 2 3	People are **content** when they do not have enough to eat. **Yes** **No**	What makes you content? _____ _____ _____ _____
❺ greedy (grē-dē) *noun* **Rating:** 1 2 3	When people are **greedy**, they want to have more than they need. **Yes** **No**	Are greedy people likeable? Why or why not? _____ _____ _____ _____

B. Use at least two of the Key Vocabulary words. Describe two of your favorite story characters and explain why you like them.

_____

_____

_____

Writing Project

Plan a New Story Ending

Fill out the FATP chart.

FATP Chart

Form: _____

Audience: _____

Topic: _____

Purpose: _____

PREWRITE

1. **Decide What to Change** List what happened at the end of *The Eagle and the Moon Gold* in the first column. Then write what will happen in your new story ending.

Actual Story Ending	New Story Ending

2. **Organize Your Ideas** Use the storyboard below to draw pictures and write sentences to tell your new story ending. Tell events in the order that they happen.

Storyboard

↓

↓

Draft a New Story Ending

Write a new story ending for *The Eagle and the Moon Gold*. Use your storyboard.

1. Write a sentence about the first event that starts your new story ending.

2. Write each of the following events in your new story ending. Write them in the order in which they happen.

Name _____

Revise a New Story Ending

PRACTICE REVISING

Read and revise this new story ending. Make a list of the order of events.

Order Of Events

1. _____

2. _____

3. _____

4. _____

5. _____

6. _____

7. _____

Eagle told Gwa to leave, but Gwa would not. He kept gathering more and more gold. As he lifted Gwa, all of the gold fell. So Eagle grabbed Gwa. Eagle carried Gwa back to Earth. He told Yaoh what had happened. Gwa returned to Earth with no gold. Both men remained friends for life. Yaoh was a kind man. He gave Gwa a present.

8. What is unclear? _____

9. Mark your changes on the draft. To move words, use this mark: ⌒.
   To add words, use this mark: ∧.

REVISE YOUR DRAFT

Read your new story ending aloud to a partner. Mark your changes on p. 85.

Edit and Proofread a New Story Ending

Editing and Proofreading Marks	
∧	Add.
℘	Take out.
⌢	Replace with this.
⬯	Check the spelling.
≡	Capitalize.
/	Make lowercase.
⁋	Make a new paragraph.

CHECK FOR QUOTATION MARKS

Proofread the sentences. Correct errors in using quotation marks. Mark your changes.

1. "Gwa said", Eagle, take me to the moon.

2. Why do you need to go to the moon?" asked Eagle.

3. "I want to gather gold" like Yaoh did, answered Gwa.

4. I will take you, said Eagle."

5. Eagle warned, "You must leave before the sun rises.

6. I cannot promise that, said Gwa.

PRACTICE EDITING AND PROOFREADING

Edit and proofread this new story ending. Mark your changes.

Checklist
❑ End marks
❑ Spelling
❑ Quotation marks

Eagle took Gwa to the (mon.)

"Hurry!" said Eagle. "The sun will rise (soun.) We must leave before it does. If we do not we will melt." Gwa did not listen to Eagle. He kept gathering more and more gold.

Eagle yelled, "We must go now " Gwa looked up and (sa) the sun. Gwa tried to run to Eagle. He was too hot to move. Eagle flew to grab Gwa and all the gold just in time. They both flew back (doun) to Earth.

"We almost both died, said Eagle. "I hope you have learned your lesson."

"I have, said Gwa. And he took just enough gold to live a quiet life. He gave the rest away to the poor

EDIT AND PROOFREAD YOUR NEW STORY ENDING

Now edit and proofread your new story ending on p. 85.

Mind Map

Use the Mind Map to show the different areas in which people can reach for their "personal best." As you read the selections in this unit, add new ideas you learn about setting goals for a personal best.

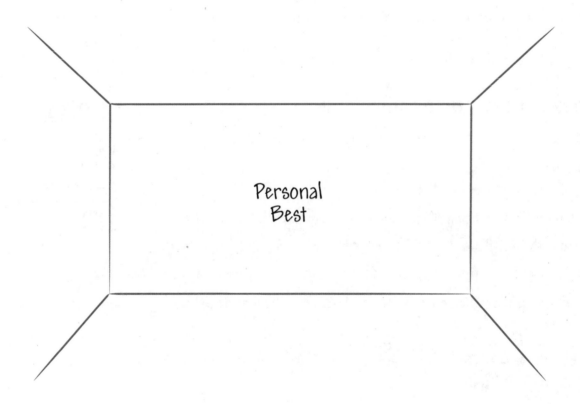

Personal
Best

Language Development

About the Body

▶ **Language: Ask for and Give Information**

▶ **Vocabulary: The Body**

Read the question. Complete the answer. Use words from the chart.

The Body	
skeleton	stomach
heart	nerves
lungs	brain
muscles	

What Body Parts Do		
help you move	pumps blood	tells your body how to act
sense feelings	digests food	breathe air

1.

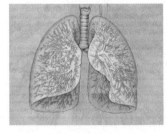

What do nerves do?

They __sense feelings_____ .

2.

What does the brain do?

It _____ .

3.

What do muscles do?

They _____ .

4.

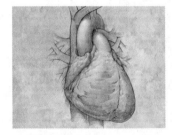

What does the heart do?

It _____ .

5.

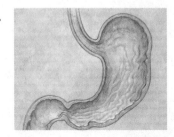

What do the lungs do?

They _____ .

6.

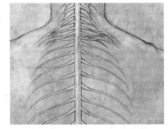

What does the stomach do?

It _____ .

Language Development

Name _____

Our Workout Routine

▶ Grammar: Present Tense Verbs

Use present tense verbs to tell what happens all the time.

Each morning we **meet** at the pool.
We always **swim** one mile.
We **stretch** before every swim.
Every day we **exercise** together.

cheer	play	race	ride	wear	go

Complete each sentence. Use verbs from the box.

1. We _____race_____ every week.

2. People always _____ for us.

3. Each Saturday the girls _____ soccer.

4. They _____ their uniforms during every game.

5. Every day I _____ to the park.

6. I always _____ as fast as I can.

Language Development

Meet the Athletes

▶ **Vocabulary: Sports**

▶ **Language: Express Thanks**

A. Look at each picture and read the sentence below it. Name what you see. Use words from the box.

scoreboard	hoop	racket	tennis ball
trophy	net	fans	coach

They play basketball.

Wendy plays tennis with her friends.

B. Your team just won a trophy for one of the games above. Write a thank-you speech. Thank your coach and the fans.

Thank you _____ for _____ .

We want to _____ .

Our coach _____ .

We also _____

_____ .

Language Development

Name _____

Watch Us Play

▶ **Grammar: Pronouns**

Use the correct pronoun when you talk about a person, place, or thing.

Use these pronouns to tell who does the action.

I	you	he	she	it	we	they

He took the ball.

Use these pronouns after an action verb or after a word like *to*, *for*, or *with*.

me	you	him	her	it	us	them

He ran with **it**.   They chased **him**.

Complete each sentence. Add the correct pronoun.

1. Our coach told _____us_____ what to do.
   (us / we)

2. Marco ran down the field.

   I passed the ball to _____ .
   (him / her)

3. He got the ball. He got _____ and ran.
   (it / you)

4. The other team chased Marco.

   _____ ran as fast as they could.
   (They / Them)

5. Marco scored! _____ won the game!
   (Us / We)

6. Later, we thanked the other team. We thanked

   _____ because they played well.
   (them / they)

Identify Main Idea and Details

▶ Sum It Up

Read the paragraph about Ann. Then use the main idea and details diagram.
Write the main idea and details.

> Ann's goal is to keep healthy. One thing Ann does to stay healthy is walk
> to school every day. She also eats plenty of fruits and vegetables. Ann also
> makes sure she gets lots of sleep each night.

Main Idea and Details Diagram

Main Idea

Detail	Detail	Detail

Language and Literacy

High Frequency Words, Part 1

A. Read each word. Then write it.

1. friends _____

2. asked _____

3. walked _____

4. trees _____

5. air _____

B. Answer the question.

6. Which words have **s**?

_____friends_____   _____   _____

C. Work with a partner. Follow the steps.

- Read aloud each new word in the box.

- Your partner writes the words.

- Have your partner read the words to you.

- Now you write the words on the lines below.

- Read the words to your partner.

7. _____

8. _____

9. _____

10. _____

11. _____

Name _____

High Frequency Words, Part 2

A. Read each word. Then write it.

1. talked _____

2. if _____

3. even _____

4. while _____

5. such _____

B. Answer the question.

6. Which words have four letters?

_____*even*_____   _____

C. Work with a partner. Follow the steps.

- Read aloud each new word in the box.

- Your partner writes the words.

- Have your partner read the words to you.

- Now you write the words on the lines below.

- Read the words to your partner.

7. _____

8. _____

9. _____

10. _____

11. _____

Words with Hard and Soft *c*

A. Name each picture. Write the name.

1.

_____ city _____

2.

_____

3.

_____

4.

_____

5.

_____

6.

_____

B. Now read the story. Circle the words with *c*. Write them in the chart in the correct column. Write each word one time.

Be a Winner

What (can) you do to win a race? You can work hard. Each day you can practice. Is there a safe park in your city or town? You can run there every day.

You can also take care of your body. You can eat good foods like carrots and cereal. Don't eat things like candy and cake. Drink lots of water. Aim for at least 6 cups a day.

What if you don't win the race? You still win by keeping your body in good shape.

7. _____ race _____	11. _____
8. _____	12. _____
9. _____	13. _____
10. _____	14. _____
	15. _____
	16. _____

Language and Literacy

Words with Hard and Soft *c* or *g*

A. Read each word. Find the picture that goes with the word. Write its letter.

1. gum └   2. garden ___   3. gem ___   4. race ___

5. city ___   6. goat ___   7. cones ___   8. cent ___

9. gate ___   10. cut ___   11. pages ___   12. cap ___

A.    B.    C.    D.

E.    F.    G.    H.

I.    J.    K.    L.

B. Name each picture below. Find the word or words in which the *c* or *g* makes the same sound. Write the words on the lines.

13.    14.    15.    16.

___ cones   _____   _____   _____

_____   _____   _____   _____

_____   _____   _____

_____

Language and Literacy

Name _____

Words with Short *oo*

A. Name each picture. Write the name.

1.

cookies

2.

_____

3.

_____

4.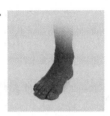

_____

B. Now read the story. Circle the words with *oo*. Write them in the chart. Write each word one time.

A New (Cookie)

I baked a new kind of cookie. First I looked at a cookbook, and then I took out what I needed. I stood at the table, where I poured and mixed. Finally, I put the cookies in the oven. Then I closed the book. My brother ran in with his football. He looked in the oven, but I shook my head. "Not yet," I said. He sat in the eating nook to wait. When the cookies were done, he took a bite. "These cookies are so good," my brother said. I love to make new things.

5. cookie	10. _____
6. _____	11. _____
7. _____	12. _____
8. _____	13. _____
9. _____	14. _____

Language and Literacy

Words with /o͝o/ or Silent Consonants

A. Name each picture. Write the name.

1.

cookies

2.

_____

3.

_____

4.

_____

5.

_____

6.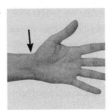

_____

7.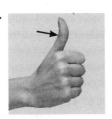

_____

8.

_____

B. Now read the story. Circle the words with /o͝o/ or silent consonants. Write them in the chart. Write each word one time.

My Very Best

I love to play (football.) I was a good player, but Coach said, "I know you can do better." So one day I walked to the library to get a book about football. I stood in the sports section a long time and looked at many books. Finally, I took one that had lots of tips: how to dodge other players, throw, and even how to keep your knees from getting wrecked. Thanks to that book, I don't do anything wrong now. Coach and my friends give me the thumbs up!

9. ___football___	15. _____
10. _____	16. _____
11. _____	17. _____
12. _____	18. _____
13. _____	19. _____
14. _____	20. _____

Build Reading Fluency

▶ Phrasing

A. When you read, pause between groups of words that go together.

> Tents were set up / in a field / by the trees.// It became an Olympic village.//

B. Listen to the story. When you hear a short pause, write a / . When you hear a long pause, write // .

Example: About 3,000 athletes, / coaches, / and volunteers / came from around the state. //

> ### Summer Games Are a Big Hit
>
> The Special Olympics State Summer Games were such a big hit this weekend at Bridge Park. About 3,000 athletes, coaches, and volunteers came from around the state. Tents were set up in a field by the trees. It became an Olympic village. People walked to other tents and talked with each other.
>
> The rock band Thumbs Up was asked to give a concert at the edge of the park to open the games. A huge crowd came to see the band. Some lucky fans even got to go on stage and sing with the band.

C. Now read the passage to a partner. Use the marks you made to read groups of words together.

Learn Key Vocabulary

Action Shots: Key Vocabulary

A. Study each word. Circle a number to rate how well you know it. Then complete the chart.

Rating Scale	**1** I have never seen this word before.	**2** I am not sure of the word's meaning.	**3** I know this word and can teach the word's meaning to someone else.

▲ **Athletes compete** in a skating race.

Key Words	Check Understanding	Deepen Understanding
❶ athlete (ath-lēt) *noun* **Rating:** 1 2 3	A professional **athlete** does not spend much time training. **Yes** **No**	What makes a good athlete? _____ _____ _____ _____
❷ compete (kum-pēt) *verb* **Rating:** 1 2 3	When people **compete** in a contest, they want to win. **Yes** **No**	What good things can happen when people compete in sports? _____ _____ _____ _____
❸ female (fē-māl) *adjective* **Rating:** 1 2 3	Only **female** swimmers race in the Olympics. **Yes** **No**	Name a female athlete you admire. _____ _____ _____ _____

Name _____

This **photograph** shows a **female athlete** in action. ▶

Key Words	Check Understanding	Deepen Understanding
❹ **male** (māl) *adjective* **Rating:** 1 2 3	Major league baseball teams are all **male**. Yes No	Describe a male athlete you admire. _____ _____ _____ _____
❺ **photograph** (fō-tō-graf) *noun* **Rating:** 1 2 3	A **photograph** can catch people doing amazing things in sports. Yes No	Describe a photograph that you like. _____ _____ _____ _____

B. Use at least two of the Key Vocabulary words. Tell about a time that you played a sport or exercised. How did you feel? What would a photograph of you look like?

_____

_____

_____

Plan a Procedure

Fill out the FATP chart.

FATP Chart

Form: _____

Audience: _____

Topic: _____

Purpose: _____

PREWRITE

1. **Choose a Topic** List the exercises that you know how to do. Then circle the one that you can explain well.

   _____   _____

   _____   _____

2. **Organize Ideas** Exercises must be done in order. Think about each step. Write each step in a sequence chain.

Exercise _____

1.

↓

2.

↓

3.

↓

4.

Draft a Procedure

Write a procedure on how to do an exercise. Use your sequence chain.

Step 1:

Step 2:

Step 3:

Step 4:

Revise a Procedure

PRACTICE REVISING

Read this procedure. Take out any details that do not belong. To take out text,
use this mark: ✐.

Play H-O-R-S-E Basketball

Step 1: Stand by the basket and try to make a shot. Dribble the ball if you want.

Step 2: The next player stands where you stood and shoots the same basket. If she doesn't

make it, she gets the letter H. If she makes it, she stands anywhere and takes another shot.

Step 3: You stand where the other player stood and try to make her shot. If you don't make it,

you get the letter H. This game can make you tired. If you make the shot, you get the next shot.

Step 4: Keep playing until someone misses five shots to spell *HORSE*. The first player to spell

HORSE loses.

What information is not needed? _____

Mark your changes. To take out text, use this mark: ✐.

REVISE YOUR DRAFT

Read your paper aloud to a partner. Mark your changes.

Edit and Proofread a Procedure

CHECK FOR CAPITAL LETTERS

Proofread the sentences below. Correct capitalization errors.
Mark your changes.

1. first, get on your hands and knees on a mat.

2. make sure your knees are under your hips and your hands are
   under your shoulders.

3. Drop your head down and arch your back up toward the ceiling.

4. bend your back toward the floor and look up.

5. finally, return to a straight back.

Editing and Proofreading Marks	
∧	Add.
℘	Take out.
⌃	Replace with this.
⬭	Check the spelling.
≡	Capitalize.
╱	Make lowercase.
¶	Make a new paragraph.

PRACTICE EDITING AND PROOFREADING

Edit and proofread this procedure. Mark your changes.

> ### How to Throw a (Futball)
>
> **Step 1:** Get a (futball) hold it in one hand. Put your (thum) on one
> side and your four fingers on the other.
>
> **Step 2:** Pick a (plase) to throw the ball. That is my target. Have
> someone stand there.
>
> **Step 3:** Move your hand behind your head. (Lok) at our target.
>
> **Step 4:** Quickly bring your hand forward. release the ball. Bend
> your (rist) to follow through.

Checklist
- ❑ Pronouns
- ❑ Spelling
- ❑ Capitalization

EDIT AND PROOFREAD YOUR PROCEDURE

Now edit and proofread your procedure on p. 104.

Mind Map

Use the Mind Map to show what you know about the United States. As you read the selections in this unit, add new ideas you learn about places and people in the United States.

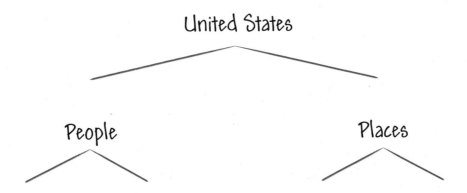

Who Built America?

▶ **Language: Ask and Answer Questions**

▶ **Vocabulary: American History**

Write a question for each answer. Use questions from the box.

Who sent them there?	What did they build?
Where did they land?	Where did they explore?
When did their trip start?	When did they cross the sea?
Who sailed to America?	What did they study?

The Pilgrims sailed from England to America.

1. _Who sailed to America?_____

The Pilgrims sailed to America.

2. _____

They crossed the sea in 1620.

3. _____

They landed in Plymouth.

4. _____

They built a colony.

Lewis and Clark explored the West for President Jefferson.

5. _____

They explored the West.

6. _____

President Thomas Jefferson sent them.

7. _____

Their trip started in 1804.

8. _____

They studied the land and animals.

Language Development

People of America

▶ Grammar: Questions with *How?* and *Why?*

You can use the words *how* and *why* to ask a question.

Use *how* to ask about the way people do something.

> **How** did some explorers travel?
> Some explorers traveled on horseback.

Use *why* to ask for a reason.

> **Why** did they ride horses?
> They rode horses **because** horses moved well and fast on rough land.

You can use *because* to answer a question with *why*.

Read each answer. Then write two questions to go with the answer.

Pioneers traveled slowly because their wagons were full and heavy.

1. How _did pioneers travel_____?

2. Why _____?

Pioneers used wood to build their homes because there were a lot of trees.

3. How _____?

4. Why _____?

Some explorers traveled in boats because it was the easiest way to travel.

5. How _____?

6. Why _____?

Language Development

Our Natural Treasures

▶ **Vocabulary: Landforms and Bodies of Water**

▶ **Language: Give Directions**

A. Look at the map. Name each landform or body of water. Use words from the box.

mountain	plains	ocean	river	lake

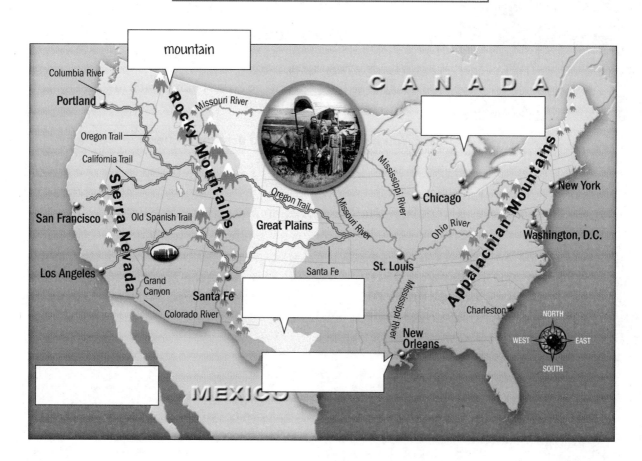

B. Read each sentence. Use the map to give directions.

1. Tell the pioneers how to go from Los Angeles to Santa Fe.

   Go east on the _Old Spanish Trail_____ . Cross the _____ .

   Keep going _____ to Santa Fe.

2. Tell the pioneers how to go from New Orleans to Portland.

   Go north along _____ to St. Louis. Go west on the

   _____ . Cross the _____ . Keep going

   _____ to Portland.

Language Development

An American Explorer

▶ **Grammar: Capitalization: Proper Nouns**

A proper noun names a particular person, place, or thing.

John Muir

Capitalize the proper names of:	Examples
countries, cities, and states	John Muir walked across **America**. He walked from **Indianapolis**, **Indiana**, to **Cedar Key**, **Florida**.
bodies of water	Muir explored **Glacier Bay**, Alaska.
landforms	**Muir Glacier** was named after John Muir.

Write each sentence again. Capitalize the proper nouns.

1. John Muir was born in dunbar, scotland, in 1838.

   John Muir was born in Dunbar, Scotland, in 1838. _____

2. Later he moved to portage, wisconsin, near beautiful fountain lake.

   _____

3. Muir walked from indiana to the gulf of mexico.

   _____

4. He studied plants and animals in yosemite valley, by the sierra mountains of california.

   _____

5. Muir explored parts of canada and alaska.

   _____

6. He studied forests in russia, india, and other countries.

   _____

Classify

▶ Sum It Up

Read about some famous Americans. Then fill in the category chart.

Famous Americans

- **Jonas Salk** was a scientist. He found a vaccine for polio, an illness that made many people sick.

- **Sandra Cisneros** is the author of many books. One of her best-known books is *The House on Mango Street*.

- **Laura Ingalls Wilder** was born in 1867. She and her family were pioneers. She wrote books based on her life.

- **César Chávez** helped farmworkers. He was an important labor leader.

- **John Wesley Powell** was a geologist, someone who studies the earth. He was also an explorer.

- **"Big Annie" Clemenc** was a labor leader. She helped people who worked in mines.

Category Chart of Famous Americans

Category	Examples
writers	
scientists	
labor leaders	

Name _____

High Frequency Words, Part 1

A. Read each word. Then write it.

1. state   _____

2. than   _____

3. high   _____

4. million   _____

5. form   _____

B. Answer the questions.

6. Which words have **i**?

_____high_____   _____

7. Which words have **t**?

_____   _____

C. Read each sentence. Choose a word from the box above. Then write it in the sentence.

8. Some caves are bigger _____ others.

9. Mammoth Cave is in the _____ of Kentucky.

10. The cave is under a _____ ridge of limestone.

11. Mammoth Cave is over one _____ years old.

12. Rivers under the ground _____ lakes inside the cave.

Mammoth Cave

High Frequency Words, Part 2

A. Read each word. Then write it.

1. sea   _____

2. near   _____

3. miles   _____

4. explore _____

5. earth   _____

B. Answer the questions.

6. Which words have **ea**?

_____sea_____   _____   _____

7. Which words start with **e**?

_____   _____

C. Read each sentence. Choose a word from the box above.
Then write it in the sentence.

8. Caves are hollow places in the _____ .

9. Caves are found inland and by the _____ .

10. Mammoth Cave is _____ the city of Bowling Green.

11. The cave is over 340 _____ long.

12. People like to _____ Mammoth Cave.

Name _____

Multisyllabic Words

A. Read each word. Write how many syllables it has.

1.

crown

___1___

2.

cactus

_____

3.

fifty

_____

4.

salt

_____

5.

badge

_____

6.
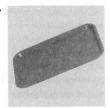
children

_____

7.

tray

_____

8.

hundred

_____

B. Now read the story. Circle the words with two syllables. Write each word in the chart. Then write the syllables in the word. Write each word one time.

The Old Days

My class went to a (hamlet) near Boston. A

hamlet is a small town. We learned how children

and their folks lived in the past. In the hamlet,

actors dress in costumes and do things by hand.

We watched a girl in a long dress churn butter. We

saw a man make nails. Life was hard hundreds of

years ago. When we got back to school, we had a

contest to see who knew the most facts.

Word	Syllables	
9. hamlet	ham	let
10.		
11.		
12.		
13.		
14.		
15.		
16.		
17.		

Language and Literacy

Name _____

Multisyllabic Words

A. Read each word. Write how many syllables it has.

1.
music

__2__

2.
wagon

_____

3.
knife

_____

4.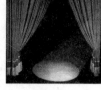
stage

_____

5.
wrist

_____

6.
planet

_____

7.
city

_____

8.
asleep

_____

B. Now read the story. Then read each word in the chart.
Write the syllables in the word.

Niagara Falls

Niagara Falls is near Buffalo, New York.

Last week, my mom and I went to visit the

falls. We stayed in a cozy cabin. We rode up the

river in a boat. The waterfalls amazed me. The

roar of the falls is so loud! The falls are about

175 feet high. They formed about 12,000 years

ago. Next time, you should come along!

Word	Syllables	
9. visit	_vis_	_it_
10. cozy	_____	_____
11. cabin	_____	_____
12. about	_____	_____
13. ago	_____	_____
14. along	_____	_____

Build Reading Fluency

▶ Intonation

A. Some sentences tell something. Other sentences ask something.

> This sentence tells something. It ends with a period.
>
> These layers sit one on top of the other, like pancakes.
>
> This sentence asks a question. It ends with a question mark.
>
> What could be more exciting than to go back a million years in time?

B. Listen to the different kinds of sentences.

> ### Deep Canyon
>
> What could be more exciting than to go back a million years in time? A visit to the Grand Canyon in the state of Arizona will take you there. It took the Colorado River millions of years to cut through the land and form the Grand Canyon.
>
> The river cut so deep into the earth that you can see nine thick layers of rock. These layers sit one on top of the other, like pancakes. The bottom layer is the oldest. At this level, you may see some of the oldest rocks on Earth.

C. Now read the sentences to a partner. See how your reading improves!

Learn Key Vocabulary

Name _____

The Big Southwest: Key Vocabulary

A. Study each word. Circle a number to rate how well you know it. Then complete the chart.

Rating Scale	**1** I have never seen this word before.	**2** I am not sure of the word's meaning.	**3** I know this word and can teach the word's meaning to someone else.

▲ There are **miles** of land and water to **explore** in the Southwest.

Key Words	Check Understanding	Deepen Understanding
❶ **states** (stāts) *noun* Rating: 1 2 3	Maine and Rhode Island are the two largest **states** in the United States. Yes No	Describe two states you would like to visit. _____ _____ _____ _____
❷ **explore** (ek-**splor**) *verb* Rating: 1 2 3	The United States has many caves to **explore**. Yes No	Describe a place you would like to explore. _____ _____ _____ _____
❸ **miles** (mīlz) *noun* Rating: 1 2 3	The Mississippi River is less than a **mile** long. Yes No	Name some places that are about a mile from our school. _____ _____ _____ _____

Name _____

There are **miles** of desert in the Southwest. ▶

Key Words	Check Understanding	Deepen Understanding
❹ **culture** (**kul**-chur) *noun* **Rating:** 1 2 3	Mexican **culture** contributes a lot to California. **Yes** **No**	Tell two things about the culture of your family. _____ _____ _____ _____
❺ **cowboy** (**kow**-boi) *noun* **Rating:** 1 2 3	A **cowboy** usually works in just one place. **Yes** **No**	Tell one thing a cowboy does, or tell how a cowboy looks. _____ _____ _____ _____

B. Use at least two of the Key Vocabulary words. Describe one feature of the Southwest that you would like to learn more about and why.

_____

_____

_____

Writing Project

Plan a Biographical Sketch

Fill out the FATP chart.

PREWRITE

1. **Collect Ideas** List names of some famous people you would like to learn more about. Circle the one you want to write about.

_____   _____   _____

2. **Gather Facts** Use books and the Internet to find the answers to the research questions. Write the answers. You can write more research questions on a separate piece of paper.

Question: When was _____ born?

Answer:

Question: Where does _____ live?

Answer:

Question: Why is _____ famous?

Answer:

Question: How has _____ helped people?

Answer:

3. **Organize Information** What is the most important fact or idea about your person? This will be your main idea. Write your main idea and details in the chart below.

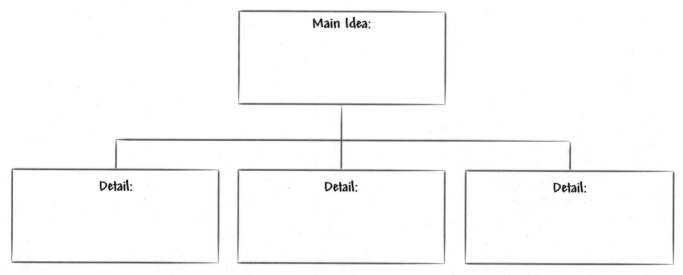

Main Idea:

Detail: Detail: Detail:

Draft a Biographical Sketch

Use your facts and your organizer as you write.

1. Write a title.

2. Write a **topic sentence** that tells the person's name and what he or she did.

3. Add the **details**.
   - Tell **when** and **where** the person lived.
   - Tell **why** the person is famous.
   - Tell **how** the person helped the United States.

Revise a Biographical Sketch

PRACTICE REVISING

Read this biographical sketch. Make sure there is a clear topic sentence and details. To add text, use this mark: ∧.

Main Idea: Roberto Clemente was a good athlete.

Details: born in Puerto Rico in 1934; died in a plane crash in 1972

Details: first Hispanic American in Baseball Hall of Fame; won 2 World Series with Pittsburgh Pirates

Details: died while flying to help people after earthquake in Nicaragua

Roberto Clemente

Roberto Clemente was a good athlete. Roberto was born in Puerto Rico in 1934. He was a great baseball player. He helped the Pittsburgh Pirates win two World Series. He is in the Baseball Hall of Fame. Roberto died in an airplane crash when he was going to help people after an earthquake.

What details could be added? Mark your changes. To add text, use this mark: ∧.

REVISE YOUR DRAFT

Read your paper aloud to a partner. Mark your changes.

Edit and Proofread a Biographical Sketch

Editing and Proofreading Marks	
∧	Add.
℘	Take out.
∧	Replace with this.
⬭	Check the spelling.
≡	Capitalize.
/	Make lowercase.
¶	Make a new paragraph.

CHECK FOR CAPITAL LETTERS AND DATES

Proofread the sentences. Correct capitalization errors.
Check commas in dates. Mark your changes.

1. John Adams was the second president of the united states.

2. He was born on October 30 1735, in massachusetts.

3. He helped thomas Jefferson write the Declaration of Independence.

4. After the Revolutionary War, general george Washington became president.

5. John Adams was his vice president.

6. In March 1797, John Adams became President.

PRACTICE EDITING AND PROOFREADING

Edit and proofread this biographical sketch. Mark your changes.

Checklist
- ❑ Proper Nouns
- ❑ Spelling
- ❑ Dates

dr. Martin Luther King, Jr., was a leader in the Civil Rights Movement. He was born January 15 1929. He (orgized) many great civil rights protests, including a march to washington and the Montgomery bus boycott. He gave great speeches. In April 1968, Martin Luther King, Jr., was shot. It was a great loss. Today we celebrate the life of Martin Luther King, Jr., every January.

EDIT AND PROOFREAD YOUR BIOGRAPHICAL SKETCH

Now edit and proofread your biographical sketch on p. 121.

Mind Map

Use the Mind Map to show what you know about growing, selling, and serving food. As you read the selections in this unit, add new ideas you learn about producing food and getting it to market.

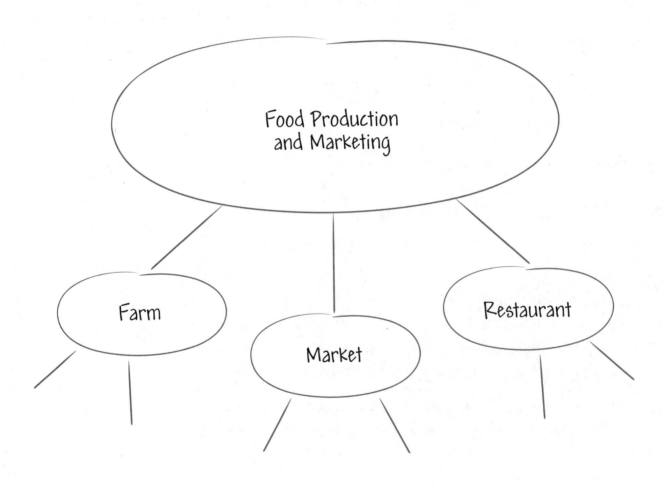

The Market Price

▶ **Language: Buy or Sell an Item**

▶ **Questions:** *How Many? How Much?*

A. Study the word boxes.

Questions
How many oranges are in a bag?
How much is one bunch of grapes?
How many peppers can I buy for $1.00?
How much do the carrots cost?

Answers
You can buy 3 peppers.
There are twelve in a bag.
The carrots are 50¢ a pound.
A bunch of grapes costs $1.00.

Questions

Use *how many* to ask about things you can count.

How many carrots are in a pound?

How many apples can I buy for $3.00?

Use *how much* to ask about a price.

How much do the peppers cost?
How much are the tomatoes?

B. What do the people say? Write questions and answers from the boxes.

Down on the Farm

▶ **Vocabulary: Farming**

▶ **Language: Give Information**

A. Name what you see in each picture. Use words from the box.

rows	crop	seedlings	farmer	tractor	soil	crate

rows

B. Complete each sentence. Tell about the pictures above.

1. The _____ farmer _____ plows the field.

2. He waters the _____ .

3. The farmer drives a _____ .

4. The tractor makes long _____ in the field.

5. Workers harvest the _____ .

6. They pack each _____ with lettuce.

Name _____

Tell the Person or Thing the Sentence Is About

▶ **Grammar: Subjects and Word Order**

The subject tells whom or what the sentence is about. It is usually a noun.

My family goes out to dinner.

The food looks good.

My father does not know what to order.

Spaghetti is usually his favorite dish.

A. Read each sentence. Underline the subject.

1. <u>My mother</u> talks to the server.

2. The server says we should try the steak.

3. The kitchen is very busy.

4. The food takes a long time.

5. The steak is very good.

6. My family thanks the server.

B. Complete each sentence. Add a subject.

7. _____ is my favorite restaurant.

8. _____ is a great dessert.

9. _____ likes healthy foods.

10. _____ cooks a good breakfast.

11. _____ drinks a lot of water.

12. _____ taste great!

Tell What the Subject Is Doing

▶ **Grammar: Predicates and Word Order**

The predicate tells what the subject of the sentence is doing, or what is happening. The predicate has a verb.

The big lunch is ready.

The chef puts out the food.

The chili looks so good.

The corn smells sweet.

People fill up their plates.

A. Read each sentence. Underline the predicate.

1. People <u>stand in line</u>.

2. A girl takes tomatoes.

3. A boy gets chili.

4. A mother feeds her baby.

5. The food tastes great.

6. Everyone thanks the chef.

B. Complete each sentence. Add a predicate.

7. Vegetables _____ .

8. Candy _____ .

9. Hamburgers _____ .

10. My favorite dessert _____ .

11. A chef _____ .

12. Restaurants _____ .

Language Development

Make Comparisons

▶ **Sum It Up**

A. Read about Ben's garden and Mary's garden. Tell how Ben and Mary's gardens are alike. Tell how they are different. Use the comparison chart.

Ben's Garden

Ben plants corn and peas. His brother helps him plant. Ben waters his garden every day. He picks the vegetables by hand, and he eats them with his family. He gives some of the vegetables to his neighbors.

Mary's Garden

Mary plants flowers. She plants them all by herself, and she waters them every day. She picks the flowers by hand. Mary decorates her home with the flowers. She shares them with her neighbors.

Comparison Chart

	Ben's Garden	**Mary's Garden**
crops	Ben plants corn and peas.	Mary plants flowers.
planting		
watering		
picking		
eating		
sharing		

B. Read each question. Write the answers.

What do Ben and Mary do that is the same?

1. They both ___water their gardens every day___ .

2. They both _____ .

3. They both _____ .

How are Ben and Mary different?

4. Ben _____, but Mary _____ .

5. Ben _____, but Mary _____ .

6. Ben _____, but Mary _____ .

Language and Literacy

Name _____

High Frequency Words, Part 1

A. Read each word. Then write it.

1. weigh	_____
2. beautiful	_____
3. special	_____
4. own	_____
5. any	_____

B. Read the clue. Write the word in the chart. Then write the word again in the sentence.

What to Look For	Word	Sentence
6. rhymes with **say**	w e i g h	Pumpkins can ___weigh___ 20 pounds.
7. ends with **ful**	__ __ __ __ __ __ __ __ __	My berries are _____ .
8. starts with **sp**	__ __ __ __ __ __ __	Fall is a _____ time.
9. means "belongs to me"	__ __ __	I want my _____ garden.
10. rhymes with **many**	__ __ __	There isn't _____ sun.

Language and Literacy

Name _____

High Frequency Words, Part 2

A. Read each word. Then write it.

1. indoors _____
2. warm _____
3. healthy _____
4. cold _____
5. outdoors _____

B. Read the clue. Write the word in the chart. Then write the word again in the sentence.

What to Look For	Word	Sentence
6. means "inside"	i n d o o r s	I stay ___indoors___ and read.
7. is the opposite of **cool**	__ __ __ __	Plants grow in the _____ sun.
8. means "not sick"	__ __ __ __ __ __ __	The pumpkins are _____ .
9. is the opposite of **hot**	__ __ __ __	Today is windy and _____ .
10. means "outside"	__ __ __ __ __ __ __ __	I work _____ under the sky.

Name _____

Suffixes: -ly, -y

A. The suffix -ly changes an adjective to an adverb. The suffix -y changes a noun to an adjective. Read each sentence. Add -ly or -y to the word in dark type to complete the sentence.

1.

The sun is **bright**. It shines
___brightly___ .

2.

The drums are **loud**. The boy plays _____ .

3.

This room is a **mess**. It is _____ .

4.

The machine digs up **dirt**. It gets _____ .

5.

He is a **safe** rider. He rides _____ .

6.

The boy plays in the **sand**. He gets _____ .

B. Now read the story. Circle each word with the suffix -ly or -y. Write the words in the chart. Then write the root words.

In the Garden

Kim's alarm clock rang (loudly.) She still felt sleepy! She dressed quickly in old pants and tiptoed softly into the garden. It was a warm, windy day. Kim bent down and dug in the rocky soil. Suddenly her hand hit something. She dug a little more and discovered a big, brown potato. Kim pulled it out of the dirt. "It must weigh five pounds," she thought. "It could make a healthy meal for six people."

Word with -ly	Root Word
7. ___loudly___	___loud___
8. _____	_____
9. _____	_____
10. _____	_____

Word with -y	Root Word
11. _____	_____
12. _____	_____
13. _____	_____
14. _____	_____

Language and Literacy

Name _____

Suffixes: *-ful, -less*

A. The suffix *-ful* means "full of." The suffix *-less* means "without." Add *-ful* or *-less* to each word to make a new word. Write the word that goes with each picture.

1.  end _less_

2.  fear _____

3.  use _____

4.  peace _ful_

5.  grace _____

6.  harm _____

B. Now read the story. Circle each word with the suffix *-ful* or *-less*. Write the words in the chart. Then write the root words.

Sun and Wind

Mike looked at his grape vines. The hot sun beat down on the plants. A warm wind began to blow. Mike was worried because wind can be (harmful) to grapes. The wind blew for days. It seemed endless. "I hope my vines survive," Mike thought. "I wish I could do something, but I am helpless." He felt so useless. At last, the wind stopped. It was peaceful again. The grape vines still looked healthy. Mike felt very thankful.

Word with *-ful*	Root Word
7. harmful	harm
8. _____	_____
9. _____	_____

Word with *-less*	Root Word
10. _____	_____
11. _____	_____
12. _____	_____

Language and Literacy

Name _____

Prefixes: *re-, un-*

A. The prefix *re-* can mean "again." The prefix *un-* can mean "not" or "the opposite of." Add *re-* or *un-* to each word to make a new word. Write the word that goes with the picture.

1.  _re_ build

2.  _____ write

3.  _____ place

4.  _un_ lock

5.  _____ happy

6.  _____ cut

B. Now read the story. Circle each word with the prefix *re-* or *un-*. Write the words in the chart. Then write the root words.

Miller's Farm

At Miller's Farm you can (relive) the past. You can taste fresh, unsalted peanuts. You can also make your own peanut butter. First, untie a big sack and take some peanuts. Be sure to retie the sack. Take off the shells. Then, put the peanuts in a grinder. Grind the peanuts to make peanut butter. Uncover a jar and fill it. Put the cover on the jar. Refill the grinder to make more peanut butter.

Word with *re-*	Root Word
7. _____relive_____	_____live_____
8. _____	_____
9. _____	_____

Word with *un-*	Root Word
10. _____	_____
11. _____	_____
12. _____	_____

Build Reading Fluency

▶ Expression

A. Some sentences tell something. Other sentences show strong feeling.

> This sentence tells something. It ends with a period.
>
> > Greenhouses have glass walls that let the sunshine in.
>
> This sentence shows strong feeling. It ends with an exclamation mark.
>
> > Farmers plant on a big scale!

B. Listen to the different kinds of sentences.

> **Many Places to Plant a Plant**
>
> Farmers plant on a big scale! They fill huge fields with millions of seeds.
>
> Plants grow well in these open fields, but not all plants are grown there.
>
> Many plants are first grown indoors, in greenhouses and in nurseries. Unlike open fields, these shelters protect plants from too much heat or cold. They also protect young plants from harmful diseases, insects, and weeds.
>
> Greenhouses have glass walls that let the sunshine in. Plants that like heat grow inside the warm, sunny space. On really cold days, steam pipes heat and reheat the greenhouse to keep the plants healthy.

C. Now read the passage to a partner. See how your reading improves!

Learn Key Vocabulary

Name _____

Plant Power: Key Vocabulary

A. Study each word. Circle a number to rate how well you know it. Then complete the chart.

Rating Scale	**1** I have never seen this word before.	**2** I am not sure of the word's meaning.	**3** I know this word and can teach the word's meaning to someone else.

▲ Many people think plants like these flowers are **beautiful**.

Key Words	Check Understanding	Deepen Understanding
❶ **beautiful** (**byū**-ti-ful) *adjective* **Rating:** 1 2 3	A field of flowers can be very **beautiful**. Yes No	Describe a plant that you think is beautiful. _____ _____ _____
❷ **energy** (**en**-ur-jē) *noun* **Rating:** 1 2 3	Food gives people **energy** to work and play. Yes No	What things do you need the most energy for? _____ _____ _____
❸ **healthy** (**hel**-thē) *adjective* **Rating:** 1 2 3	Exercising once a year is a **healthy** habit. Yes No	Name three foods that keep you healthy. _____ _____ _____

Name _____

Broccoli is a **healthy** food that is full of **vitamins**. ▶

Key Words	Check Understanding	Deepen Understanding
❹ **oxygen** (**ok**-si-jen) *noun* **Rating:** 1 2 3	People need **oxygen** to live. **Yes** **No**	Why do living things need oxygen? _____ _____ _____ _____
❺ **vitamins** (**vi**-tuh-minz) *noun* **Rating:** 1 2 3	Fruits and vegetables are full of **vitamins**. **Yes** **No**	How does your body get vitamins? _____ _____ _____ _____

B. Use at least two of the Key Vocabulary words. Describe how plants are part of your everyday life.

_____

_____

_____

Writing Project

Name _____

Plan a Report

Fill out the FATP chart.

FATP Chart

Form: _____

Audience: _____

Topic: _____

Purpose: _____

PREWRITE

1. **Choose a Topic** Make a list of your favorite fruits or vegetables.

_____   _____

_____   _____

Choose two crops to compare and contrast.

2. **Collect Facts** Use books and the Internet to find facts. Write your facts on cards.

3. **Organize Ideas** Use the Venn Diagram to compare and contrast the two crops.

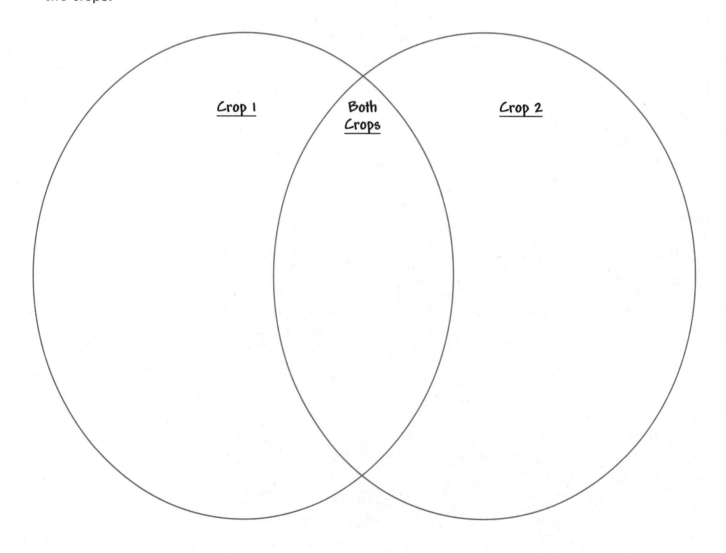

Crop 1   Both Crops   Crop 2

Draft a Report

Use your Venn diagram to write a draft of your report.

1. Write a **title**. Name the crops you will compare.

2. Write a **topic sentence**. Name the two crops again.

3. Turn the ideas in your Venn diagram into sentences.

- Tell how the crops are **alike**. Use the words *both* and *and*.

- Tell how the crops are **different**. Use the word *but*.

- Include **details**. Tell how the crops look and taste. Tell how they grow and are harvested.

Crop Report: _____ and _____

Revise a Report

PRACTICE REVISING

1. Read this report. Make sure the writer stayed on the topic and included clear details.

Crop Report: Apples and Oranges

Apples and oranges are both fruits, but they are very different.

Apples grow in all fifty states. Oranges only grow where there is

warm weather all year. Apples can be red, green, or yellow. All

apples have seeds on the inside. Strawberries have seeds on the

outside. Apples grow on trees. Oranges grow on trees. Apples are

grown in orchards, and oranges are grown in groves. Some kinds of

oranges have seeds, and some are seedless.

---

2. Mark your changes. To take out text, use this mark: ℘.
   To move text, use this mark: ↶◯.
   To add text, use this mark: ∧.

REVISE YOUR DRAFT

Read your paper aloud to a partner. Mark your changes.

Edit and Proofread a Report

CHECK FOR CAPITAL LETTERS

Proofread the sentences. Correct capitalization errors.
Mark your changes.

1. I can get both avocados and almonds at the fresno farmers' market.

2. Both Almonds and Avocados grow on trees.

3. Both almonds and avocados are grown in california.

4. Most avocados are grown in san diego county.

5. Almonds are grown between the cities of Red Bluff and bakersfield.

6. You can find avocados and almonds in most cities in the United states.

7. Whether you live in new jersey or Arizona, eat avocados and almonds.
   They are both very good for you!

Editing and Proofreading Marks	
∧	Add.
℘	Take out.
⌒	Replace with this.
◯	Check the spelling.
≡	Capitalize.
╱	Make lowercase.
¶	Make a new paragraph.

PRACTICE EDITING AND PROOFREADING

Edit and proofread this report. Mark your changes.

> ### Crop Report: Cabbage and Lettuce
>
> Cabbage and lettuce look alike but are very different vegetables. Cabbage is grown in new york and many other places. Most lettuce is grown in california and arizona. Lettuce must be eaten right after it is picked. It is (quicky) sent to stores. can be stored cabbage. (Unnlike) lettuce, cabbage can be stored for five months. Cabbage and lettuce look alike but taste very different.

Checklist

❑ Subject and predicate
❑ Spelling
❑ Proper Nouns

EDIT AND PROOFREAD YOUR REPORT

Now edit and proofread your report on p. 139.

Mind Map

Use the Mind Map to show what you know about stars. As you read the selections in this unit, add new ideas you learn about who or what stars are and where they can be found.

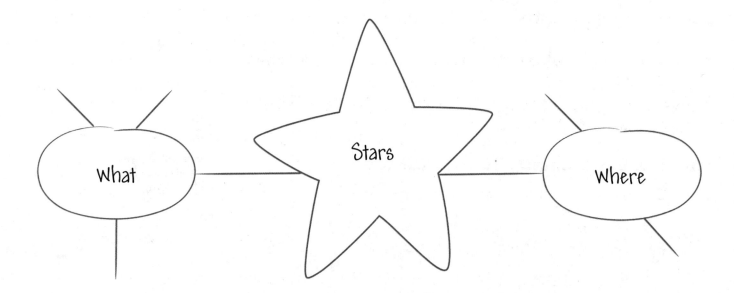

Do You Agree?

▶ **Language: Agree and Disagree**

▶ **Vocabulary: Idioms**

> **Idioms**
> No way!
> no good
> one of a kind
> leave all other
>   bands behind

A. What can you say to agree or disagree? Study the chart.

I Agree	I Disagree
You are right.	No way!
That is so true!	You are wrong.
I think so, too.	That isn't true.
You bet!	I don't think so.

B. Read each opinion. Do you agree or disagree? Write your opinion. Use some of the words in the chart.

1.

Rock bands play the best music.

That is so true! Rock bands leave all other bands behind!

_____

2.

The guitar is the most important part of a rock band.

_____

_____

_____

3.

Most kids like to dance to music.

_____

_____

_____

4.

Country music stars sing better than rock stars.

_____

_____

_____

You Will Be a Star!

▶ Grammar: Future Tense Verbs and Contractions

A verb in the future tense tells what will happen later, or in the future.

Here are some ways to show the future tense.

will + verb	Our band **will play** new songs next week.
am + **going to** + verb **are** + **going to** + verb **is** + **going to** + verb	I **am going to sing.** You **are going to play** the drums. The concert **is going to be** great!
we'll + verb	We <u>will</u> write new music. **We'll write** new music. The contraction for *we will* is *we'll*.
won't + verb	We <u>will not</u> play our old songs. We **won't play** our old songs. The contraction for *will not* is *won't*.

Complete each sentence. Tell about the future. Use words from the box.

will find
is going to join
won't forget
will write
won't play
is going to be

1. Miguel _____ is going to join _____
   a jazz band.

2. He _____
   rock music.

3. Sally _____
   a singer.

4. She _____
   the words to the song.

5. The boys _____ music.

6. They _____
   someone to play it.

Language Development

Outer Space

▶ **Vocabulary: Space**

A. Name what you see in each picture. Use words from the box.

galaxy	shooting star	star	Moon	Sun	planets

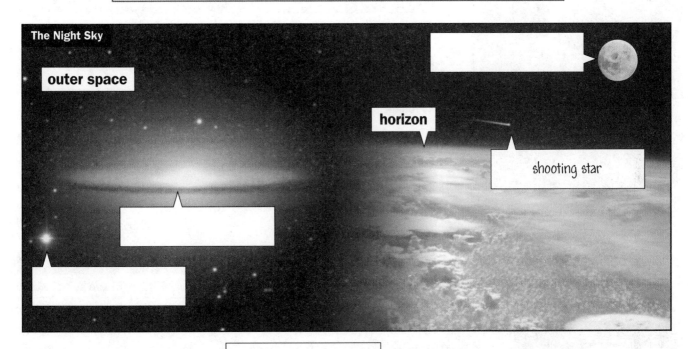

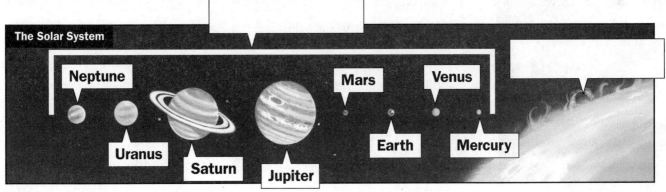

B. Complete each sentence. Write facts about the night sky and the solar system.

1. _____Mars_____ is the fourth planet from the Sun.

2. Jupiter, Mars, and Venus are _____ in our solar system.

3. The name of our planet is _____ .

4. _____ is the biggest planet.

5. The night sky has billions of _____ .

Language Development

They Went to the Moon

▶ Grammar: Verb Tenses

The tense of a verb shows when the action happens.

Tense	Tells	Example
Past	what happened earlier	Astronauts **landed** on the Moon in 1969.
Present	what is happening now	Astronauts still **explore** space.
Future	what will happen later	Some day they **will visit** Mars. They **are going to do** experiments there.

Complete each sentence. Use verbs from the chart.

Past	Present	Future
visited	visits	are going to visit
used	use	will use

1. Astronauts _____*visited*_____ the Moon for the first time on July 20, 1969.

2. On that day, they _____ a spaceship called a lunar module.

3. Today they _____ a space shuttle to travel in space.

4. It _____ a space station.

5. In the future, they _____ Mars.

6. Astronauts _____ new machines to explore Mars.

The Moon Glows

▶ Grammar: Verb Tenses

The tense of a verb shows when the action happens.

Tense	Tells	Example
Past	what happened earlier	Last week, the Moon **was** full.
Present	what is happening now	Tonight I **see** part of the Moon.
Future	what will happen later	In three weeks, the Moon **will be** full again. The sky **is going to be** very bright.

Complete each sentence. Write the correct form of the verb.

1. Every night, Dana _____likes_____ to look at the sky.
   (like)

2. Sometimes she can't _____ the Moon.
   (see)

3. Two weeks ago, there _____ no Moon.
   (is)

4. Last night, clouds _____ it.
   (cover)

5. Tomorrow Dana _____ to see the Moon.
   (try)

6. She hopes it _____ in the sky.
   (glow)

7. Dana is going to _____ more about the Moon and stars.
   (learn)

8. She is going to _____ a picture of the night sky.
   (draw)

Identify Goal and Outcome

▶ Sum It Up

Read about how Xenia became a rock star. Then complete the goal-and-outcome map.

> Xenia loved music. She wanted to become a rock star. Every day she practiced the guitar. Then she began to play her music in concerts. Many people went to her concerts. Everybody loved her music. They bought her CDs. Xenia was a famous rock star!

Goal-and-Outcome Map

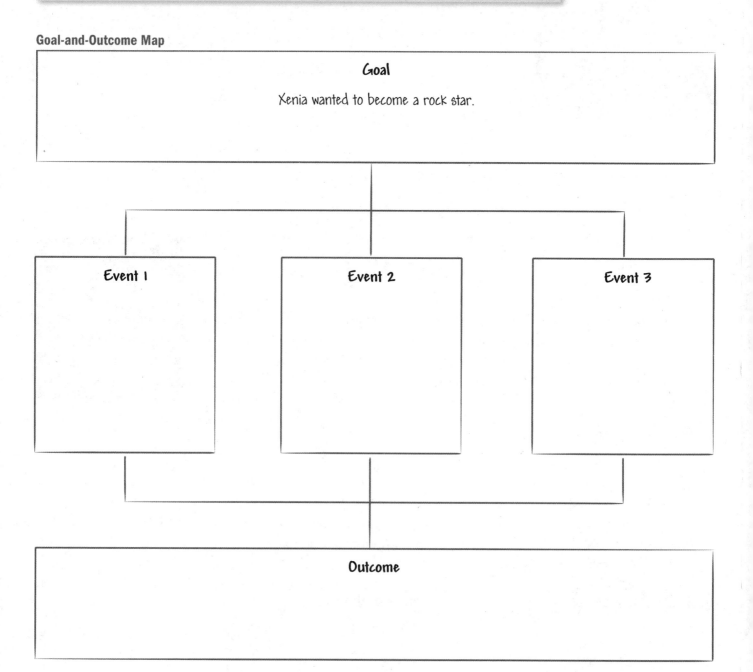

Goal

Xenia wanted to become a rock star.

Event 1

Event 2

Event 3

Outcome

High Frequency Words, Part 1

A. Read each word. Then write it.

1. show   _____

2. right   _____

3. close   _____

B. Read each question. Find the new words in the box. Write the words on the lines.

4. Which words name actions?

    ___show___   _____

5. Which word is the opposite of "left"?

    _____

6. Which word can be both a verb and a noun?

    _____

7. Which word can mean "near"?

    _____

8. Which words can be adjectives?

    _____   _____

Language and Literacy

High Frequency Words, Part 2

A. Read each word. Then write it.

1. watch _____

2. kind _____

B. Read each question. Find the new words in the box. Write the words on the lines.

3. Which word names an action?

_____ watch _____

4. Which word is an adjective?

_____

5. Which word can be both a verb and a noun?

_____

6. Which word means "look at"?

_____

7. Which word means "type of"?

_____

Types of Syllables

A. Name each picture. Read the two words. Circle the word that names the picture.

1.

middle / (pickle)

2.

table / little

3.

circle / gentle

4.

beetle / eagle

5.

apple / able

6.

candle / huddle

7.

twinkle / title

8.

turtle / purple

B. Now read the story. Circle the words with a consonant + -le. Write them in the chart.

A Native American (Fable)

Native Americans tell stories about Coyote. In one story, Coyote sees a little star that twinkles like a candle. "Come close!" Coyote yells. "I want to dance with you." The star floats down and he grabs it. He soars like an eagle, high over Table Rock. He isn't able to hang on. His hands slip and he tumbles down. Splat! He lands by a beetle. What did Coyote learn? It's simple: You can't do everything you want.

Long Vowel in First Syllable	Short Vowel in First Syllable
9. _____Fable_____	14. _____little_____
10. _____	15. _____
11. _____	16. _____
12. _____	17. _____
13. _____	18. _____

Language and Literacy

Types of Syllables

A. Name each picture. Read the two words. Circle the word that names the picture.

1.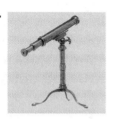
(telescope) / tolerate

2.
fourteen / fifteen

3.
reptile / record

4.
aboard / alone

5.
beneath / between

6.
remain / repeat

7.
fearful / faithful

8.
celebrate / calculate

B. Now read the story. Circle the two-syllable words. Find the vowel pattern. Write each word in the chart. Write each word one time.

Apollo (Thirteen)

In 1970, a space capsule tried to reach the moon. However, a mistake caused two air tanks to explode. No one knew the reason for the mistake. Yet the craft could not go to the moon. The astronauts had to survive, so they released the tanks. Teams on Earth watched and helped the crew succeed. They exclaimed joyfully when the astronauts got home alive.

Two Vowels Work Together	Vowel and *e* Work Together
9. _____Thirteen_____	14. _____capsule_____
10. _____	15. _____
11. _____	16. _____
12. _____	17. _____
13. _____	18. _____

Multisyllabic Words

A. Read each word. Write how many syllables it has.

1.
eagle

_____2_____

2.
unbuckle

_____

3.
faithful

_____

4.
superstar

_____

5.
telescope

_____

6.
replace

_____

7.
candle

_____

8.
unafraid

_____

B. Now read the story. Circle the words with more than one syllable. Write each word in the chart one time. Then write the syllables in the word.

The (Republic) of Blues

My band is called The Republic of Blues. A lot of faithful fans come to our shows. They love our kind of music. I play the steel drums and Clive sings. He likes to rearrange old songs, too. I like his simple love songs best. I hope he does not leave the band. I would be so unhappy. I don't think I could replace him. I hope we will both be stars one day!

Word	Syllables		
9. Republic	Re	pub	lic
10. _____	____	____	
11. _____	____	____	
12. _____	____	____	____
13. _____	____	____	
14. _____	____	____	____
15. _____	____	____	

Name _____

Build Reading Fluency

► Phrasing

A. When you read, pause between groups of words that go together.

> Winter sat / all alone.// He was huddled close to / a cold fire.//

B. Listen to the story. When you hear a short pause, write a / . When you hear a long pause, write // .

Example: In the Old Time, / Winter stayed on Earth forever.//

Fifth Moon's Story

In the Old Time, Winter stayed on Earth forever. Rain and snow fell on the land. It was quite a show. Fields and rivers were covered by snow. The Earth Children looked at their calendars. When would the cold end? They asked Sun to show kindness. "Please tell Winter to go away!"

The kind Sun went by Winter's house. Winter sat all alone. He was huddled close to a cold fire. Sun came and sat on Winter's right side. Winter recognized Sun. "Go away!" Winter shouted. He tried to push Sun out and close the door.

C. Now read the passage to a partner. Use the marks you made to read groups of words together.

Learn Key Vocabulary

Name _____

Exploring Space: Key Vocabulary

A. Study each word. Circle a number to rate how well you know it. Then complete the chart.

▲ Earth's **moon** is part of our **solar system**.

Rating Scale	**1** I have never seen this word before.	**2** I am not sure of the word's meaning.	**3** I know this word and can teach the word's meaning to someone else.

Key Words	Check Understanding	Deepen Understanding
❶ space (spās) *noun* **Rating:** 1 2 3	On clear nights, you can see stars in **space**. Yes No	From Earth, what can you see in space? _____ _____ _____ _____
❷ solar system (sō-lur **sis**-tum) *noun* **Rating:** 1 2 3	Mars is part of our **solar system**. Yes No	Name something in our solar system. _____ _____ _____
❸ rocket (**rok**-it) *noun* **Rating:** 1 2 3	A **rocket** usually takes off quietly. Yes No	Describe a rocket taking off. _____ _____ _____

Name _____

There are many planets in our **solar system**. ▶

Key Words	Check Understanding	Deepen Understanding
❹ **moon** (mūn) *noun* **Rating:** 1 2 3	Earth has just one **moon**. **Yes** **No**	Describe the way Earth's moon looks over the course of one month. _____ _____ _____ _____
❺ **astronauts** (**as**-tru-nots) *noun* **Rating:** 1 2 3	**Astronauts** wear special suits. **Yes** **No**	Would you like to be an astronaut? Tell why or why not. _____ _____ _____ _____

B. Use at least two of the Key Vocabulary words. Tell why it is important for astronauts to learn more about space.

_____

_____

_____

Plan a Diamante Poem

Fill out the FATP chart.

PREWRITE

1. **Collect Ideas** Make a list of objects found in outer space. Write space objects that can be compared in pairs.

   _____ / _____

   _____ / _____

   _____ / _____

   Circle the pair you like best.

2. **Gather Information** Use books and the Internet to find facts about the two objects you will compare. Write the facts on the cards.

   Object 1: _____

   Object 2: _____

Draft a Diamante Poem

Use your cards to write a draft of your diamante poem.

1. At the top, write a **noun** that names one thing in outer space. Write a different noun at the bottom.

2. Write 2 **adjectives** that describe the noun at the top.

3. Write 3 **verbs** that end in **-ing**. The verbs should tell about both nouns.

4. Write 2 **adjectives** that describe the noun at the bottom.

_____
noun

_____   _____
adjective   adjective

_____ _____ _____
verb with **-ing**   verb with **-ing**   verb with **-ing**

_____   _____
adjective   adjective

_____
noun

Revise a Diamante Poem

PRACTICE REVISING

Read these diamante poems. Look for words that don't belong. Make sure the correct words are in each line. To replace text, use this mark: ⌃.

asteroid
noun

many
adjective

small
adjective

orbits
verb with -ing

moving
verb with -ing

round
verb with -ing

stars
adjective

large
adjective

planet
noun

manned space station
noun

manned
adjective

scientific
adjective

experimenting
verb with -ing

orbiting
verb with -ing

learn
verb with -ing

power
adjective

reusable
adjective

space shuttle
noun

REVISE YOUR DRAFT

Read your poem aloud to a partner. Mark your changes on your draft. To replace text, use this mark: ⌃.

Edit and Proofread a Diamante Poem

PRACTICE EDITING AND PROOFREADING

Edit and proofread these diamante poems. Mark your changes.

Moon

big   object

(shineing)   turning   (flowting)

(sparkley)   small

star

Mercury

smallest   first

travel   orbiting   revolve

largest   (fiveth)

Jupiter

EDIT AND PROOFREAD YOUR DIAMANTE POEM

Now edit and proofread your diamante poem on p. 158.

Timed Reading Chart

How many words did you read correctly for each selection? Complete the chart to show your scores for each day.

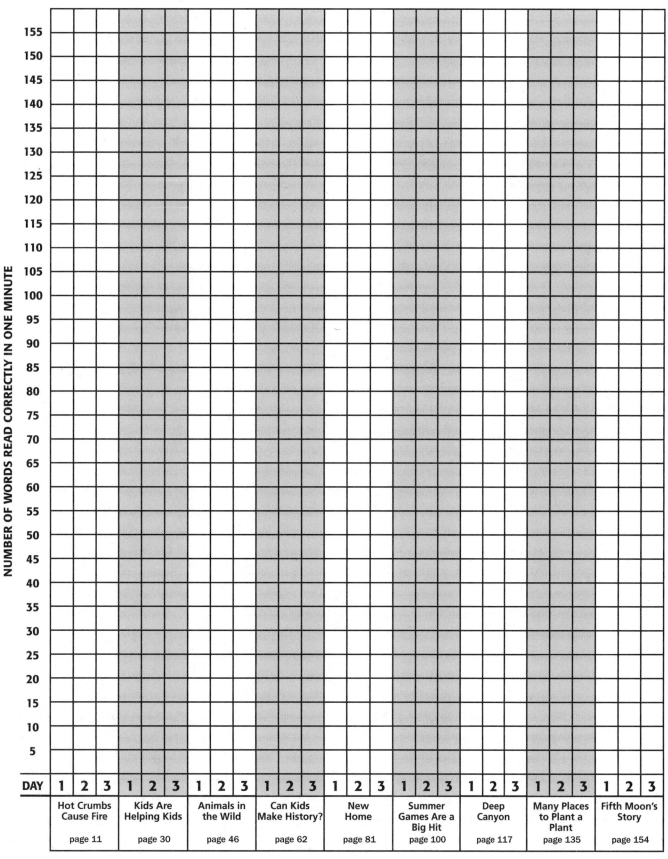

NUMBER OF WORDS READ CORRECTLY IN ONE MINUTE

DAY	1	2	3	1	2	3	1	2	3	1	2	3	1	2	3	1	2	3	1	2	3	1	2	3	1	2	3
	Hot Crumbs Cause Fire			Kids Are Helping Kids			Animals in the Wild			Can Kids Make History?			New Home			Summer Games Are a Big Hit			Deep Canyon			Many Places to Plant a Plant			Fifth Moon's Story		
	page 11			page 30			page 46			page 62			page 81			page 100			page 117			page 135			page 154		

Decodable Stories

Contents

Fold

Long Vowels: ie, igh; ui, ue

RESCUE at the BEACH

Thanks! You tried to warn me. You are a great lifeguard!

Words with Long Vowels: ie, igh; ui, ue

blue	high	right	suit
bright	might	sign	true
fight	rescue	skies	tried

High Frequency Words for Unit 1

| almost | never |

Unit 1 Here to Help

The skies are blue and the water feels great. Ann and Kim plan to have a good day at the beach. They meet Deb on the sand.

Hi, Deb, I like your bright red suit.

Thanks, Ann! It's my lifeguard suit.

2

This time, Ann listens. She does what Deb tells her. Deb meets Ann and helps her to the shore.

You gave me a fright! I'm glad you are safe.

7

INSIDE Decodable Book 1: Long Vowels: *ie, igh; ui, ue*

Ann is surprised that Deb is a lifeguard. Kim isn't.

Ann tries to fight the wave. Another high wave is coming. Deb yells to Ann. She tells Ann what to do.

Ann is in a rush to get in the water and start surfing. She is between the waves and the rocks. She doesn't see the sign about the rocks. Deb tells her to watch out.

Watch out for the rocks on your right! A wave might take you too close.

DANGER KEEP AWAY FROM ROCKS

4

Ann doesn't listen to Deb. Then a big wave takes her close to the rocks. She needs help! Deb runs as fast as she can.

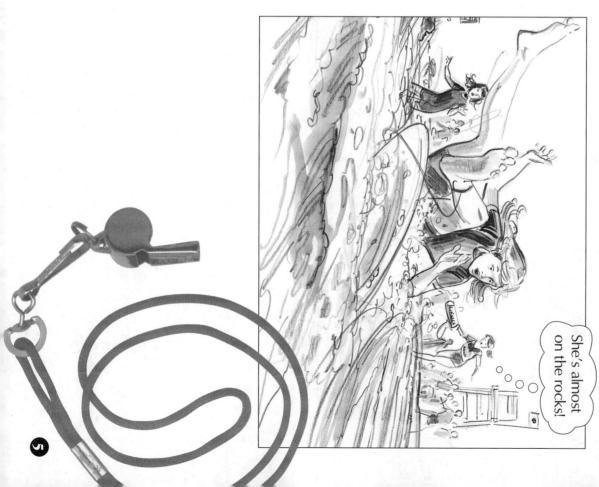

She's almost on the rocks!

5

R-Controlled Vowels

Community Bulletin Board

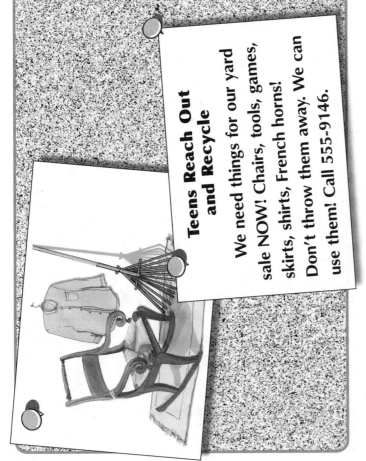

Teens Reach Out and Recycle

We need things for our yard sale NOW! Chairs, tools, games, skirts, shirts, French horns! Don't throw them away. We can use them! Call 555-9146.

Words with R-Controlled Vowels

art	curb	hurt	shirts
artist	dirt	March	skirts
barn	fern	Mark	star
Bert	first	market	start
birds	for	New York	third
car	hard	north	turn
chirp	homework	park	world
concert	horns	porch	yard

High Frequency Words

country	house	now

Unit 2 Make a Difference!

All around the world, teens use their time and skills to help others. Teens in this country are no different. American teens use their skills to make the world a better place. Look around your city for a community bulletin board like the one on these pages. Find your own way to make a difference!

2

Start the Year Right!

Come and hear how to protect birds. Join **The Bird Group,** Sundays at 2:00 p.m., on the porch of The Country House, 524 Third Street (near Hassan's Market).

Chirp!

7

Are you a star at math?

Help at **The Homework** Place.

Get $6.00 an hour.

861 First Street

Ask for Bert.

CONCERT IN THE BARN
MAY 1

Bring your earplugs!

The Hard Rock Boys are doing a concert to raise money for three children hurt in a fire this year. The star of the show will be **Mark Jones.** This is your last chance to hear him play before he moves to New York.

Car Wash
$5.00
We get the dirt off!

**Help our school band take
a trip to Bear Mountain.**

Bring your car to Park School,
10 Park Drive, on March 30.

(Go north on Fern Lane. Turn right on Park Drive. Park at the curb.)

Be an Artist for the Day
Make Art
in the Park

March 31

You can **paint**. You can **weave** or make a **clay pot**. Funds will be used to add a room to Deerfield Senior Center.

The Perfect Moose

The perfect moose may live for as long as 12 years.

Words with *R*-Controlled Syllables

antlers	member	under
expert	perfect	water
forests	swimmers	winter

High Frequency Words

also	because	four
away	called	mountains

Unit 3 Our Living Planet

The moose is a member of the deer family. The white-tailed deer, the elk, and the caribou are part of this same family. Members of the deer family live in many parts of the world.

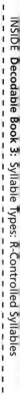

white-tailed deer

elk

caribou

moose

2

A grown moose does not fear attack because it is so big. A wolf pack or a bear may attack a calf or a moose that is sick, but not one that is grown and strong.

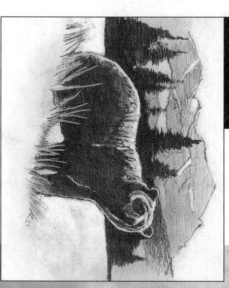

brown bear

wolf

7

Moose live in northern mountains and forests. A mother is called a cow. A baby is called a calf. Calves are born in the spring and stay with the mother for a year. Then the mother chases them away, and they must survive on their own.

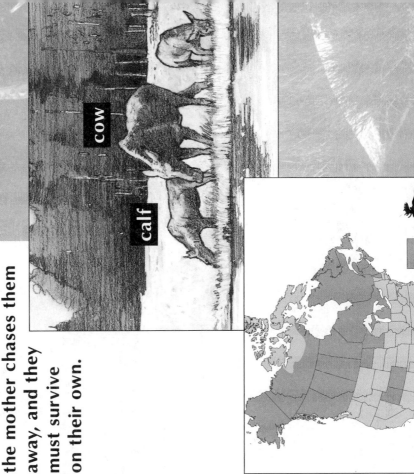

calf   cow

Where moose live in North America

☐ =

③

Moose like water and are expert swimmers. They wade in ponds and lakes to eat the plants that grow under the water. They also eat twigs and shrubs on land. Moose will not hunt animals, but some animals hunt them.

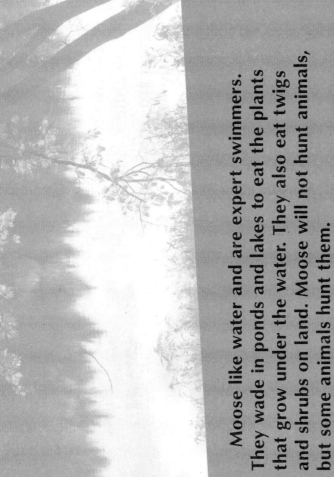

⑥

Moose like to live alone. They do not form herds like other members of the deer family. When there is a lot to eat, three or four moose may stay together for a while.

4

The male, or bull, has big antlers. He uses the antlers to fight other bulls during mating time. Bulls shed the antlers in the winter and grow new antlers in the spring.

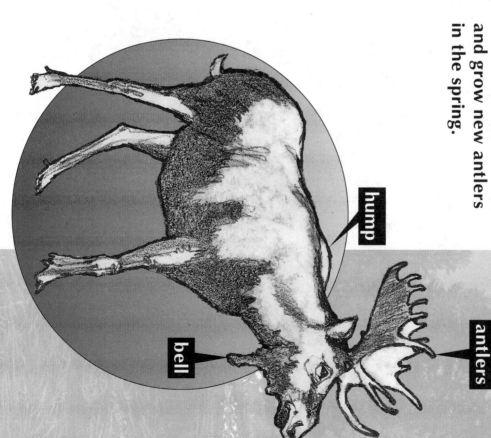

hump

bell

antlers

5

Kathy's Diary

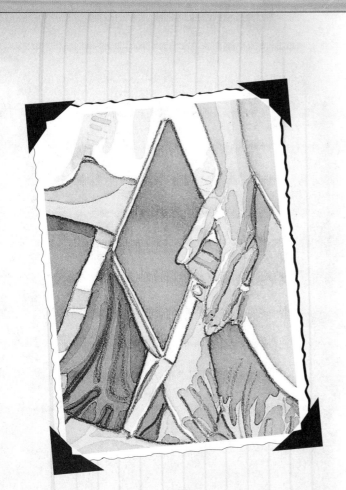

Words with y		
army	Grady	lucky
daddy	happy	my
diary	Italy	silly
entry	Kathy	sky
		study

High Frequency Words		
away	called	four
been	ever	life
		over
		words

Unit 4 Past and Present

In 1960, Kathy is all grown up. She has two children of her own. She reads her diary to them. Her kids like to hear about life in the 1940s. It seems like a long time ago, but the words in Kathy's diary bring the past to life.

Back in 1945, Kathy Grady started a diary. She wrote about her life during that time.

Each page Kathy wrote is called an entry. Here are some entries from Kathy's diary.

My dad is home!

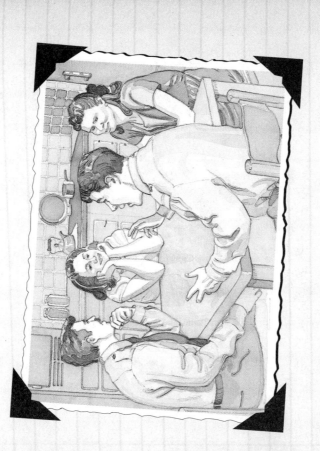

One of his Army buddies is
with him. We feel so lucky to
have him back! Mom is happier
than ever. She is going to make
french fries and hamburgers.
They are Dad's favorite foods.

Daddy went to Italy three
years ago. He is in the Army
Air Force. He flies a big plane
called a B-42.

This picture shows my dad with
some of his buddies. Dad is the
second man on the right. We miss
him so much!

3

Some nights we sit and study the sky. We are watching for our boys to fly home. Many of them have been away for four years!

People say the war may end soon! We all wait for that happy day.

The war is over! People are yelling and waving flags. You can hear their cries of joy. We all act silly. Mom is playing music and dancing.

I rushed out to get a newspaper. Dad can read it when he gets home.

MORNING NEWS
★ THE WAR ENDS! ★

Victory!

A Pinch of Salt

The neighbors clapped with joy. At last, they all sat down to eat. They chatted and joked and ate lots of stew, just as they always did.

Enjoy!

Mmmm! Great stew!

The best ever!

Words with: Diphthongs and Variant Vowels

all	down	join	small
always	enjoy	joy	soon
awful	few	noon	stew
boiled	food	Paul	too
call	found	proud	town
called	frowned	salt	
crowd	house	saw	

High Frequency Words for Units 1–5

as	ever	house	made
called	few	into	over
each	found	lived	

Once there was a wise woman named Mrs. Paul. She lived in a small house at the end of town. She was not rich, but all her neighbors loved her. One morning the woman saw that her cupboard was empty. She found only a few peas to eat. She was too proud to beg, but she was too smart to stay hungry.

She put the peas into the pot. She filled the pot with water. Then she put the pot over the fire, just as she always did.

It was time for the woman to add one last thing, just as she always did. She added a pinch of salt. She stirred the pot, then tasted the stew again.

Perfect!

When the pot began to simmer and steam, she called to her neighbors.

Join me for a pot of stew!

Thank you!

We will join you!

All the neighbors heard her call. They nodded and smiled, just as they always did.

The woman tasted the stew. She frowned.

This stew tastes awful!

The neighbors smiled and waited, just as they always did.

Soon, a crowd of neighbors entered her house. They each added food to the pot. They added carrots, meat, onions, and more peas. They filled the pot to the brim, just as they always did.

The pot boiled over the fire. By noon, the smell of rich stew filled the small house. It made the neighbors hungry.

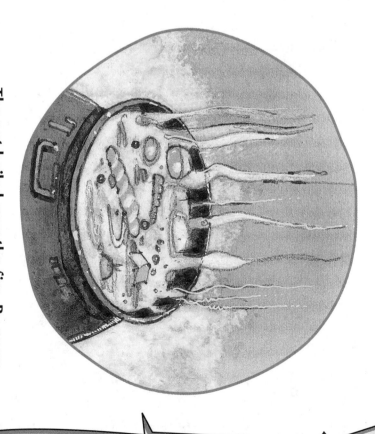

Variant Vowels and Consonants

A Good Game

Rick

Gene

Mel

Can't I just hit the puck from here?

Sure!

He skates, and he falls. He falls, and he skates. He falls twice in a row, but he's such a good sport. Gene's friends knew he would have fun at hockey!

Words with Variant Vowels and Consonants			
cage	facemask	gives	huge
can't	game	going	ice
come	Gene	good	laces
edge	get	great	twice

High Frequency Words for Units 1–6			
even	if	while	would
friends	into		

Unit 6 Personal Best

2

Gene's friends take him to the ice rink to play hockey. There are kids on the ice already. They are playing a game. This is Gene's first time on skates.

I don't know about this!

Come on. You'll do fine!

We're your friends. We'll help you.

Gene looks at the other kids. They are moving so fast! At last, Gene gets on the ice. He puts one foot in front of the other. He's on his feet, and he's skating!

7

Gene sits at the edge of the ice. While he puts on his skates, he watches the players on the ice. Some of them are huge!

Tie the laces tight.

Look how fast they're going!

Mel wants to be sure Gene is safe.

3

The boys are ready to play. Mel shows Gene the puck. Rick gives him the wooden stick.

Gene does not think he will be good at hockey.

You're going to love this game, Gene.

I can't even stand up!

Try to knock the puck into the cage.

6

4

Mel helps Gene strap on his shin guards. They will protect his knees and shins.

Strap the shin guards on tight.

Rick brings Gene some elbow pads.

Mel gives Gene a facemask.

Do I have to wear that?

Yes. You have to wear a facemask if you want to play.

Rick can't wait to get in the game.

Come on. It's a great game!

5

Multisyllabic Words

POSTCARDS from DEVEN

Arizona
New Mexico

Southwestern States

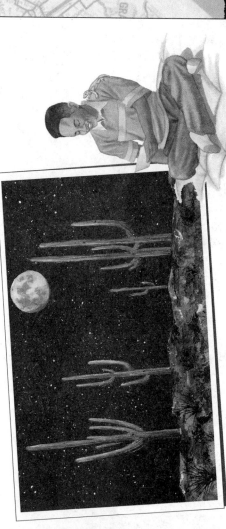

Last night we camped under a million stars! A coyote howled at the moon. Dad told funny stories about cowboys in the desert. I think we laughed for hours. I want to come back here soon.

See you next week. I have a lot of pictures to show you.

Multisyllabic Words

amazing	cowboys	ladders	river
Anasazi	desert	midnight	skyscrapers
awake	Deven	music	stories
below	didn't	picture	thousands
border	dwellings	postcards	today
bridges	funny	rafting	towers
cabin	hiking	rapids	very
cooler	hundreds	reading	village
corners	jackets	relaxed	western

High Frequency Words

back	even	miles	over
could	explore	million	states
country	high	mountains	until
four	house	much	walked
Earth	into	near	

Unit 7 This Land Is Our Land

Hey, Brent! I am at Four Corners. This is the place where four states share a border. It is the only place in the U.S. like this. I stood on all four states at one time! Dad took a great picture of me.

Four Corners

Arizona

Utah

New Mexico

Colorado

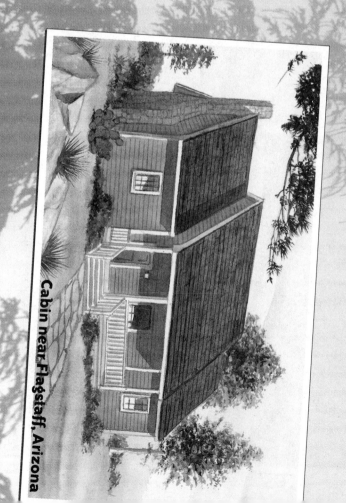

Cabin near Flagstaff, Arizona

I am reading a good book about the Anasazi. I could not put it down last night. I was awake until midnight!

Today, we just relaxed in our cabin. I was so tired. Dad got us big burritos for lunch. There's a country-western music show later. I am going to dance and dance!

EXPLORE AMAZING UTAH!

Today, we went hiking in the mountains near Four Corners. It was hot in the valley below. We walked for three hours to get to the top. It's so high up there! You can see for miles! It was much cooler, too. We even had to wear our jackets.

③

White Water Rafting in Arizona

This is the most amazing place on Earth! We went rafting on the river. The red and brown canyon walls around us are taller than my house. The river took us over fast rapids. The water was very cold. It felt great in the hot sun.

⑥

4

Wow! This place is great. There are thousands of big red rocks here. Some look like skyscrapers and bridges, too. You need to see them sometime. I didn't want to leave.

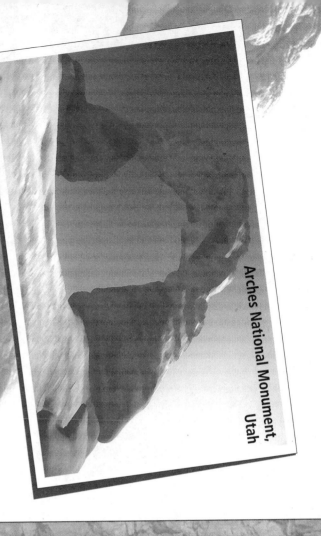

Arches National Monument, Utah

Mesa Verde, Colorado

Today, we got to explore some cliff dwellings. The Anasazi people built them hundreds of years ago. There are many rooms in the cliffs. In fact, the rooms form a village. There are ladders that go into some of the rooms. Some rooms have round towers.

5

Prefixes and Suffixes

The Orchard

Late at night, I go outside and
think about my great-grandfather.
I'm so happy to share the gift he
left my family so long ago.

Words with Prefixes and Suffixes

beautiful	finally	refill	thankful
carefully	fuzzy	reuse	tightly
countless	gently	silently	unlike
cupfuls	harmful	softly	unpack
endless	helpful	sticky	unripe

High Frequency Words

as	beautiful	friends	outdoors
any	each	healthy	special
away	few	indoors	trees
back	form	near	warm

Unit 8 Harvest Time

My family has a beautiful peach orchard. My great-grandfather planted the trees as a special gift to his family. Every summer, we all gather to pick the plump fruit from the trees. We are very thankful for the trees.

2

We boil the filled jars. This kills any harmful bacteria in the fruit. After the jars cool, we label each one.

Our canned fruit is unlike anything you buy in a store. Sometimes when we give a jar away, the people bring back the empty jar and ask for a refill!

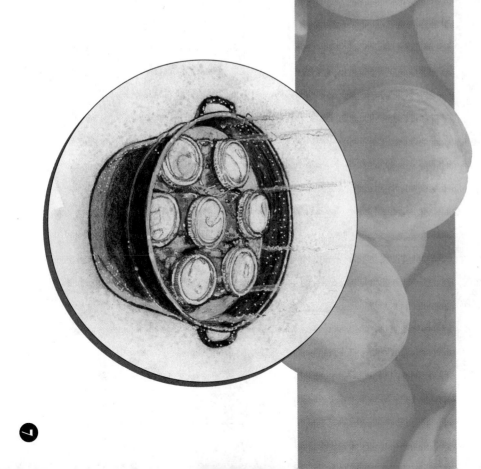

7

We wait all year for the peaches to grow. In the late winter, small pink buds appear on the trees. The flowers blossom. Then the petals fall off and float silently to the ground. In the spring, the fuzzy peaches start to form. We set up a big picnic table near the branches full of hard, unripe fruit. We all eat together under the shade of the trees.

Only a few more weeks until the peaches are ripe!

We sit and listen. The leaves flutter softly in the wind. It is like Great-grandfather's voice whispering that we will soon enjoy his gift.

3

Dad gently washes each peach. I peel the skin and remove the pits. Mom carefully packs the fruit into the jars and covers it with cupfuls of warm, sticky syrup. Then we screw on each lid tightly.

6

When summer is finally here, there is endless work outdoors. All of the family and countless friends arrive. Everyone is so helpful. We carry crates and pick the healthy fruit.

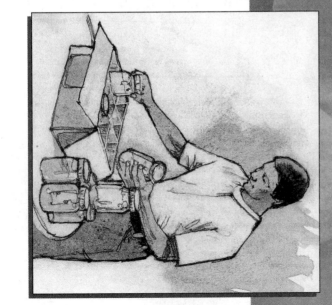

4

We have a lot of fresh peaches, so we put some in jars to enjoy in the winter.

When it's time to can the fruit, there is endless work indoors. We unpack boxes of glass jars that we reuse from year to year. We still have a few jars from when Great-grandmother canned peaches years ago!

5

Meteor Shower

The Geminids will come again next year, too. Look for them. If the sky is clear, you will be amazed, too!

Multisyllabic Words

another	excited	Latin	suddenly
beneath	fantastic	looking	surprised
celebrate	Geminids	planet	surrounds
crashes	going	really	very
darkest	happen	season	whizzing
eleven	hardly	shooting	winter
enjoy	hundreds	shower	

High Frequency Words

as	cold	if	right
because	earth	into	show
called	friends	know	watch
close	from	often	

Unit 9 Superstars

Fold

It's the middle of the night on December 13. It is winter, the darkest season of the year. My friends wonder what I am going to show them. They grumble as we trudge up the steep hill.

What a fantastic way to celebrate the darkest season of the year! My friends and I will always remember this night.

I smile and lead them up the hill. I did not tell them what is going to happen. I want them to be surprised. I know they will enjoy the show. I check my watch. It's eleven p.m. The night sky will soon be filled with hundreds of shooting stars, or meteors, whizzing past the earth. I can hardly wait.

Look! Look!

Suddenly hundreds of meteors begin to shoot across the sky. It's like a fireworks display! My friends do not grumble anymore. They are really glad they came. We huddle beneath blankets and watch the amazing show.

Meteors are bits of space dirt. They hurtle through space at great speeds. Some pass very close to Earth. They burn up in the layer of gas that surrounds the planet. Meteors look like bright balls of fire as they burn. Most burn out and then fall to the earth as dust.

Sometimes a meteor does not burn up and crashes into Earth with a great bang! That does not happen very often.

The meteor shower begins right on time. My friends are excited to see the first shooting star. I do not tell them that there will be more— many more.

Look! A shooting star!

Yes! There's another one! Where do they come from?

These meteors are called Geminids because they appear to come from a group of stars called Gemini. I look in the sky for that group of stars. I tell my friends that Gemini means "The Twins" in Latin. I point to The Twins in the night sky.

Photographs

2 (tl) Art Explosion, (tr) Sean Murphy/Getty Images, (bl) Robert Brenner/PhotoEdit, (br) John Paul Endress. **3** (tl) Bonnie Kamin/PhotoEdit, (tc) David Young-Wolff/PhotoEdit, (tr) Robert Brenner/PhotoEdit, (ml) David Young-Wolff/PhotoEdit, (mc) Sean Murphy/Getty Images, (mr) Terry Vine/Blend Images/Jupiter Images. **4** (tl) Ed Bock/Corbis, (ml) Gary Buss/Getty Images, (mr) David Young-Wolff/PhotoEdit. **5** (t) David Buffington/Getty Images, (b) Billy E. Barnes/PhotoEdit. **9** Row 1: (l, m) Artville, (r) Liz Garza Williams. Row 2: (l) Digital Vision, (m) Duomo/Corbis. Row 3: (m) Artville, (r) Liz Garza Williams. **10** Row 1: (l) Artville, (m) John Paul Endress, (r) Artville. Row 2: (l) J. A. Kraulis/Masterfile, (m) John Foster/Photo Researchers, inc (r) John Paul Endress. Row 3: (m) J. A. Kraulis/Masterfile, (r) John Paul Endress. **12** (t) Dale Spartas/Corbis. **13** (t) Forestier Yves/Corbis Sygma. **22** (t) Bettmann/Corbis, (mr) Corbis. **26** Row 1: (l) VisionsofAmerica/Joe Sohm/Getty Images, (lm) Jules Frazier/Getty Images, (rm) Artville, (r) Liz Garza Williams. Row 2: (l) Artville, (ml) Stockbyte, (mr) Siede Preis/Getty Images, (r) Chat Roberts/Corbis/Jupiter Images, (bc) Artville, (br) Siede Preis/Getty Images. **27** Row 1: (l) John Paul Endress, (ml) Getty Images, (mr) Jess Alford/Getty Images, (r) Artville. Row 2: (l) Barbara Penoyar/Getty Images, (ml) Siede Preis/Getty Images, (mr) Getty Images, (r) Lee Snider/Corbis. Row 3: (m) Siede Preis/Getty Images, (r) Getty Images. Row 4: (m) Artville, (r) Barbara Penoyar/Getty Images. **28** Row 1: (l) Getty Images, (ml) Plush Studios/Getty Images, (mr) Chat Roberts/Corbis/Jupiter Images, (r) Getty Images. Row 2: (l) Liz Garza Williams, (ml) Stockbyte, (mr) Getty Images, (r) Jess Alford/Getty Images. Row 3: (mr) Plush Studios/Getty Images, (r) Jess Alford/Getty Images. Row 4: (mr) Chat Roberts/Corbis/Jupiter Images, (r) Liz Garza Williams. **29** Row 1: (l) Ryan McVay/Getty Images, (ml) Paul Dance/Getty Images, (mr) Francisco Erize/Bruck Coleman Inc., (r) Ryan McVay/Getty Images. Row 2: (l, ml) Getty Images, (mr) Artville, (r) Jules Frazier/Getty Images. Row 3: (m) Ryan McVay/Getty Images, (r) Paul Dance/Getty Images. Row 4: (m) Ryan McVay/Getty Images, (r) Artville. **31** (tr) Flip Schulke/Corbis. **32** (tr) Hulton-Deutsch Collection/Corbis. **38** (t-b) Digital Stock, Getty Images, Gabe Palmer/Corbis, Getty Images, Getty Images. **40** (bg) Glen Allison/Getty Images, (fg) Digital Stock. **45** Row 1: (l) Digital Vision/Getty Images, (ml) 1999-2000 Getty Images, Inc., (mr, r) John Paul Endress. Row 2: (l) Freeman Patterson/Masterfile, (ml) David Sailors, (mr) Getty Images, (r) Brian Hagiwara/PhotoPix/Jupiter Images. **47** (t) age fotostock/SuperStock. **48** (t) Hold Studios International Ltd/Alamy. **54** (l) Getty Images, (m) Bettmann/Corbis, (r) Passage To Freedom: The Sugihara Story permission arranged with Lee & Low Books. **55** (tl) Corbis, (bc) Bettmann/Corbis. **56** (tl) Getty Images, Row 1: (l, r) Getty Images. Row 2: (l) Burke/Triolo Productions/FoodPix/Jupiter Images, (r) Bettmann/Corbis. Row 3: (l) Getty Images, (r) FPG/Getty Images. **60** Row 1: (l) Peter Gridley/Getty Images, (m) Visions of America/Joe Sohm/Getty Images, (r) Corbis. Row 2: (l) Paul Thomas/Getty Images, (m, r) John Paul Endress. Row 3: (m) Corbis, (r) VisionsofAmerica/Joe Sohm/Getty Images. **63** (t) Galen Rowell/Corbis. **64** (t) David Crausby/Alamy. **71** (ml) Liz Garza Williams. **77** Row 1: (l) Barbara Penoyar/

Getty Images, (m) Artville, (r) John Smyth/SuperStock. Row 2: (l) John Paul Endress, (m) Carl & Ann Purcell/Corbis, (r) Digital Stock. Row 3: (m) Carl & Ann Purcell/Corbis, (r) John Paul Endress. **78** Row 1: (l) Barbara Penoyar/Getty Images, (ml) C Squared Studios/Getty Images, (m) Getty Images, (mr) John Smyth/SuperStock, (r) Carl & Ann Purcell/Corbis. Row 2: (l) Ron Chapple/Thinkstock/Jupiter Images, (ml) John Paul Endress, (m) Getty Images, (mr) Artville, (r) Peter Byron/PhotoEdit. Row 3: (l) Getty Images, (ml) Ken Giese/SuperStock, (m) Digital Stock, (mr) Liz Garza Williams, (r) Tony Freeman/PhotoEdit. **79** Row 1: (l) Getty Images, (m,r) John Paul Endress. Row 2: (l) John Paul Endress, (m) Stockbyte, (r) John Foster/Photo Researchers. Row 3: (m) John Paul Endress, (r) Stockbyte. **80** Row 1: (l, ml) Getty Images, (m) Stockbyte, (mr) Artville, (r) Corbis/Jupiter Images. Row 2: (l) John Paul Endress, (ml) Riat Maas/Getty Images, (m) Mike McQueen/Getty Images, (mr) John Paul Endress, (r) David Young-Wolff/PhotoEdit. Row 3: (l) C Squared Studios/Getty Images, (ml) John Foster/Photo Researchers, (m) Ryan McVay/Getty Images, (mr) Jules Frazier/Getty Images, (r) John Paul Endress. **82** (t) Araldo de Luca/Corbis. **83** (t) Gianni Dagli Orti/Corbis. **89** (all) Artville. **90** (t-b) Tony Freeman/PhotoEdit, Ken Usami/Getty Images, Tom Carter/PhotoEdit, Stockbyte/Getty Images. **96** Row 1: (l) Digital Stock, (m) John Paul Endress, (r) Artville. Row 2: (l, m) Getty Images, (r) Ryan McVay/Getty Images. Row 3: (m) Digital Stock, (r) Getty Images. **97** Row 1: (l) Ryan McVay/Getty Images, (ml) Getty Images, (mr) Lawrence Lawry/Getty Images, (r) Digital Stock. Row 2: (l) Getty Images, (ml) Jonathan Nourok/PhotoEdit, (mr) John Paul Endress, (r) Liz Garza Williams. Row 3: (l) Artville, (ml) Getty Images, (mr) John Paul Endress, (r) GeoStock/Getty Images. Row 4: (l) Zoran Milich/Masterfile, (ml) Getty Images, (mr) Liz Garza Williams, (r) Robert Daly/Getty Images. **98** (tl) Getty Images, (tc) Getty Images, (ml) Liz Garza Williams, (mc) Getty Images, (mr) Liz Garza Williams. **99** Row 1: (l, ml) Artville, (mr, r) Getty Images. Row 2: (l, ml, mr) Getty Images, (r) Donald Specker/Animals Animals-Earth Scenes. Row 3: (mr, r) Artville. **101** (t) Duomo/Corbis. **102** (t) AP Photo/Todd Bissonette. **108** (tl, ml) Bettmann/Corbis. **109** (tl) Bettmann/Corbis. **110** (tc) Corbis. **111** (tl) Bettmann/Corbis. **113** (mr) David Muench/Corbis. **115** Row 1: (l) C Squared Studios/Getty Images, (ml) Howard Folsom/PictureQuest/Jupiter Images, (mr) Phil Borden/PhotoEdit, (r) Rita Maas/Getty Images. Row 2: (l) Getty Images, (ml) Camille Tokrud/Getty Images, (mr) Liz Garza Williams, (r) John Paul Endress. **116** Row 1: (l) Bettmann/Corbis, (ml) PhotoSphere Images/PictureQuest, (mr) Artville, (r) Robert Daly/Getty Images. Row 2: (l) Getty Images, (ml) D. Ducros/Photo Researchers, (mr) Digital Stock, (r) Digital Vision/PictureQuest. **118** (t) Jack Dykinga/Getty Images. **119** (t) David Muench/Corbis. **126** (tl) Amy Toensing, (tr) Patrick Bennett/Getty Images, (mr) ©GMEVIPHOTO/Shutterstock. **127** (tl) Jack Hollingsworth/Getty Images. **128** (tl) Jeff Greenberg/PhotoEdit. **132** (tl) Datacraft/Getty Images, (tc) John Paul Endress, (tr) Richard Hutchings/Corbis, (ml) Koolstock/Radius Images, (mc) Blend Images/Jupiter Images, (mr) Barbara Peacock/Getty Images. **133** (tl) Tom Bean/Getty Images, (tc) Bettmann/Corbis, (tr) Authur S. Aubry/Getty Images, (ml) David Young-Wolff/PhotoEdit, (mc) Bonnie Kamin/Photo Edit, (mr) Tom Brakefeld/Getty Images. **134** (tl) John Paul

Endress, (tc) Myrleen Ferguson Cate/PhotoEdit, (tr) Corbis, (ml) Image Club, (mc) Liz Garza Williams, (mr) Getty Images. **136** (t) Emmanuel Lattes/Alamy. **137** (t) Tom Mareschal/Getty Images. **143** (tl) John Paul Endress, (tr) Artville, (ml) Karen Moskowitz/Getty Images, (mr) Stockbyte/Getty Images. **144** (t-b) John Paul Endress, Steve Satushek/Getty Images, Hoby Finn/Getty Images, E. Dygas/Getty Images. **145** (tl, tr) Digital Stock, (mr) Premium Stock/Corbis, (b) NASA. **146** (t-b) Stockbyte, Getty Images. **147** (tl, r) Getty Images. **151** Row 1: (l) Artville, (ml) Getty Images, (mr) John Running, (r) Getty Images. Row 2: (l, ml, r) Getty Images. **152** Row 1: (l) Getty Images, (ml) Diego Azubel/epa/Corbis, (mr) Layne Kennedy/Corbis, (r) Steph Fowler/Brand X/Jupiter Images. Row 2: (l) David Young-Wolff/Getty Images, (ml) John Paul Endress, (mr) Tom Stewart/Corbis, (r) Bill Bachmann/PhotoEdit. **153** Row 1: (l) Getty Images, (ml) Diane Macdonald/Getty Images, (mr) Tom Stewart/Corbis, (r) Burke/Triolo Prouductions/Brand X/Jupiter Images. Row 2: (l) Getty Images, (ml) Corbis, (mr) Getty Images, (r) VCL/Spencer Rowell/Getty Images. **155** Corbis. **156** Steve A. Munsinger/Photo Researchers. **163** (bgr) Getty Images. **164** (bgl, br) Getty Images. **165** (bgl) Getty Images, (br) Liz Garza Williams. **167** (bgl) Digital Stock, (br) Artville. **171** (tl) Digital Stock. **172** (bg) Corel. **173** (bg) Digital Stock. **174** (bg) Getty Images. **187** (bg) Liz Garza Williams. **188** (bgl) Getty Images, (bgr) Digital Stock. **189** (bg) Artville. **190** (bg) Digital Stock. **191** (br) Artville. **192-194** (bg) Getty Images. **195-198** (bg) Digital Stock.

Illustrations

7 Judith DuFour Love. **19** Maurie Manning. **20, 21** Judith DuFour Love. **39, 41** Karen Morgan. **61, 70** Judith DuFour Love. **71** Lane Yerkes. **72, 73** Judith DuFour Love. **89** Artville. **91, 92, 109** Judith DuFour Love. **125** Maurie Manning. **163-166** Frank Sofo. **167-170** Marcia J. Bateman Walker. **171-174** Lee Woolry. **175-178** Ken Stetz. **179-182** Lee Woolry. **183-186** Frank Sofo. **187-190** Stephen Wells. **191-194** Lee Woolry. **195-198** Den Schofield.